Human Rights in Focus: Torture

Bradley Steffens

ReferencePoint Press®

San Diego, CA

For more information, contact:
ReferencePoint Press, Inc.
PO Box 27779
San Diego, CA 92198
www.ReferencePointPress.com

LIBRARY OF CONGRESS CATALOGING-IN-PUBLICATION DATA

Name: Steffens, Bradley, 1955–author.
Title: Human Rights in Focus: Torture/by Bradley Steffens.
Other titles: Torture
Description: San Diego, CA: ReferencePoint Press, Inc., 2018. | Series:
   Human Rights in Focus | Includes bibliographical references and index.
Identifiers: LCCN 2017021327 (print) | LCCN 2017029966 (ebook) | ISBN
   9781682822364 (eBook) | ISBN 9781682822357 (hardback)
Subjects: LCSH: Torture—Juvenile literature. | Human rights—Juvenile
   literature.
Classification: LCC HV8593 (ebook) | LCC HV8593 .S73 2018 (print) | DDC
   364.6/7—dc23
LC record available at https://lccn.loc.gov/2017021327

Contents

A Darkening World

In 1948, following the widespread human rights abuses committed against soldiers and civilians by Nazi Germany, imperial Japan, and the Soviet Union's Red Army during World War II, the newly formed United Nations (UN) issued the Universal Declaration of Human Rights. It was explicitly designed to prevent such atrocities in the future. Article 5 of the declaration includes a prohibition against torture, stating, "No one shall be subjected to torture or to cruel, inhuman or degrading treatment or punishment."[1] The nations that adopted the declaration hoped that by bringing international pressure to bear on offending governments, the UN could greatly reduce, if not eradicate, the practice of torture.

Universal Condemnation

In one sense, the UN's prohibition against torture has succeeded: The world's powers have officially renounced the use of torture in all its forms. Fifteen international agreements forbid torture, including the African Charter on Human and Peoples' Rights, the American Convention on Human Rights, the Arab Charter on Human Rights, the Cairo Declaration on Human Rights in Islam, the European Convention for the Prevention of Torture and Inhuman or Degrading Treatment, and the Inter-American Convention to Prevent and Punish Torture. Virtually every nation has formally adopted one or more of these agreements. "Torture is universally condemned, and whatever its actual practice, no country publicly supports torture or opposes its eradication,"[2] states Human Rights Watch, a nonprofit organization dedicated to protecting human rights.

Torture has not been banished in practice, however. Nations that had signed the Declaration of Human Rights in 1948 were soon conducting torture in secret around the world. In Algeria between 1954 and 1962, the French military under the command of General Jacques Massu tortured thousands of people aligned with the groups fighting for Algerian independence. In an interview in 2000, when he was ninety-two years old, General Massu admitted that French forces used torture. "Torture is not indispensable in wartime, we could have very well done without it," he told the French newspaper *La Monde.* "When I think of Algeria, it makes me very sorry, because that [torture] was part of a certain atmosphere; we could have done things differently."[3]

Great Britain also employed torture when putting down rebellions in its former colonies. In 2012 the British government admitted that its colonial administration in Kenya tortured and abused detainees during the Mau Mau uprising between 1952 and 1960, which led to that country's independence. At a hearing held to determine whether surviving torture victims could sue the British government over their treatment, Guy Mansfield, an attorney representing the government, said, "[The British government] does not dispute that each of the claimants suffered torture and other ill-treatment at the

Nazi doctors subject a prisoner to experiments with freezing temperatures at Dachau concentration camp around 1942. Atrocities like this prompted the United Nations to issue its Universal Declaration of Human Rights.

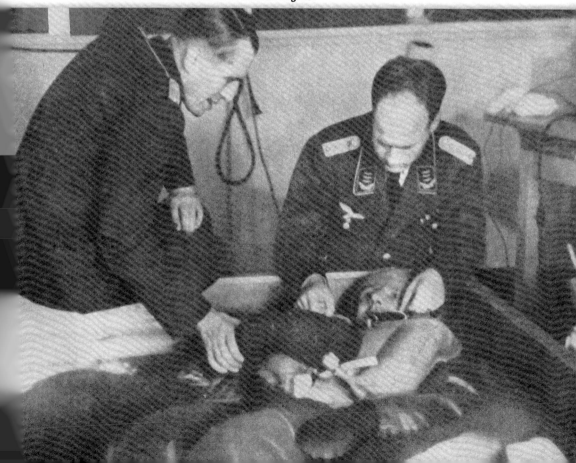

hands of the colonial administration." Speaking directly to the Mau Mau claimants present in the courtroom, Mansfield added, "I do not dispute that terrible things happened to you."[4]

One Mau Mau veteran, Paulo Nzili, who was eighty-five years old at the time of the hearing, described how he was treated by a white settler nicknamed "Luvai," which means "merciless person" in Nzili's language. "They tied both of my legs with chains and . . . pinned down both my hands," Nzili stated in sworn testimony. "Then Luvai approached me with a pair of pliers which were more than a foot long and castrated me."[5]

> "Governments around the world are two-faced on torture—prohibiting it in law, but facilitating it in practice."[7]
>
> —Salil Shetty, secretary-general of Amnesty International

Great Britain is also accused of using torture during the fight against colonial rule in Cyprus between 1955 and 1959. Petros Patrides, a Cypriot businessman, says that when he was fifteen he was detained by British forces during the uprising. Patrides says that British officers abused him in several ways, including by waterboarding him, a technique that simulates drowning. "They tied me on a bed, spread-eagled and naked, and rubbed pepper into my lips and eyelids, and my private parts," says Patrides. "They would put a piece of cloth over your nose and mouth and dip water on to it and you would feel like you were drowning. Just before you passed out they would stop and take the cloth off. And then they would start again."[6]

A Growing Scourge

In 1984 the United Nations took further action to abolish torture, adopting the UN Convention Against Torture (UNCAT). Since then, 155 nations have ratified the agreement. This has not caused the use of torture to decrease, however. In fact, human rights groups report that its use is increasing. Despite the widespread prohibition, more than half of the countries party to the UNCAT—seventy-nine nations, according to the human rights organization Amnesty International—continue to practice torture. Another forty UN member nations that never adopted the convention also engage in torture. As Salil Shetty, secretary-general of Amnesty International, puts it, "Governments around the world are two-faced on torture—prohibiting it in law, but facilitating it in practice."[7]

Chapter 1

Torture in the Twenty-First Century

In August 2015 archaeologists studying seven-thousand-year-old bones recovered from a construction site near Frankfurt, Germany, announced a startling discovery. Not only had the twenty-six men, women, and children whose remains they had found been killed, but evidence suggested they might have been tortured as well. Half of the shin bones recovered from the site had been broken at the time of the attack. "A new violence-related pattern was identified here: the intentional and systematic breaking of lower limbs," write the researchers from the University of Mainz in Germany. "The abundance of the identified perimortem [around the time of death] fractures clearly indicates torture and/or mutilation of the victims."[8]

The German discovery, known as the Schöneck-Kilianstädten mass grave, remains the oldest documented example of the systematic torture of a group. It shows that torture has been used since the advent of human history, and probably long before that. Today, torture continues to be used to punish people or force them to do things against their will.

Why Is Torture Used?

Torture uses physical and psychological pain to control a victim. This control can then be used to achieve a variety of goals, such as obtaining information or instilling fear. Gaining control over another human being affects the torturer as well, often making him or her feel superior or powerful; torturers who profoundly enjoy the suffering of others are known as sadists.

Torture is complex, and it can involve many factors and have many goals. Experiencing extreme pain causes the victim to fear more pain. That fear might cause him or her to agree to whatever demands the torturer makes. At the same time, causing the victim to give in to certain demands can give the torturer a sense of satisfaction. These are powerful emotions that the torturer might want to experience again and again.

Torture During Wartime

Although people sometimes conduct torture during times of peace and stability, most torture occurs during times of extreme conflict, when violence is commonplace, such as during war. Surrounded by death and destruction, military officers may decide to torture captives—known as prisoners of war (POWs)—to punish them or obtain information. Armies also sometimes torture civilians to obtain information or to send a message to others about what might happen to them if they oppose the military force.

For example, when forces of the Islamic State (IS), a militant group that follows an extreme doctrine of Islam, conquered parts of Syria and Iraq in 2014, its members tortured civilians. After occupying Fadiliya, a village a few miles northeast of Mosul, Iraq, IS militants tortured a local civilian named Abdel Razzaq Jalal, claiming that he was a spy. "They hung me upside down from my feet and beat me for two hours. That was on the first night," Jalal said. "They used cables, wooden sticks, and one of them— there were three or four—pistol-whipped me repeatedly on my head." The torture went on for six days and seven nights. "The second day, they lay me flat on my stomach with my hands tied behind my back. One man stood on my legs, another on my head, and they began raising my arms. I thought my chest was going to break." The IS troops urged Jalal to admit he was a spy, but he refused. "I never confessed. I knew the punishment would be death,"[9] he said. Eventually, the IS militants released Jalal, but two of his cell mates were not so fortunate. After they confessed under torture to helping direct air strikes against IS fighters, they were killed.

The ongoing Boko Haram uprising in the African nations of Nigeria, Cameroon, Chad, and Niger has also given rise to widespread torture. According to the Council on Foreign Relations, more than forty-seven thousand people have been killed in the conflict since 2011. That is when Boko Haram, an armed Islamist group, began to clash with Nigerian government security forces. According to a 2014 report by Amnesty International, the Nigerian

Masked members of the extremist militant group Islamic State parade through northern Syria. The group's members have tortured civilians both in Syria and Iraq.

government is using torture in its efforts to put down the rebellion. "Torture and other ill-treatment are routine practice in criminal investigations across Nigeria," states Amnesty International. "Many police sections in various states . . . have 'torture chambers': special rooms where suspects are tortured while being interrogated. Often known by different names like the 'temple' or the 'theatre,' such chambers are sometimes under the charge of an officer known informally as 'O/C Torture' (Officer in Charge of Torture)."[10] Aliyu, a fifty-five-year-old man who was beaten by Nigerian police, told Amnesty International, "I wasn't killed by the soldier's bullet, but I don't know if I'll survive the pain of the soldiers' stick."[11]

Rape as Torture

Throughout history, armies have used rape as a way to gain control over civilian populations. "Rapes committed in war are aimed

9

The Hook

Sam Johnson is a former Vietnam War POW who currently serves in the House of Representatives. In 2015 he described a torture device used on American pilots held in a North Vietnamese prison known as the Hanoi Hilton. The device was a meat hook that hung from the ceiling in rooms in which they were tortured. The pilots called it "the hook":

> It would hang above you in the torture room like a sadistic tease—you couldn't drag your gaze from it. During a routine torture session with the hook, the Vietnamese tied a prisoner's hands and feet, then bound his hands to his ankles—sometimes behind the back, sometimes in front. The ropes were tightened to the point that you couldn't breathe. Then, bowed or bent in half, the prisoner was hoisted up onto the hook to hang by ropes. Guards would return at intervals to tighten them until all feeling was gone, and the prisoner's limbs turned purple and swelled to twice their normal size. This would go on for hours, sometimes even days on end. Aside from leg irons and leg stocks—both of which were used on me for months and years on end—the meat hook was a favorite instrument of torture at the Hanoi Hilton.

Sam Johnson, "I Spent Seven Years as a Vietnam POW. The 'Hanoi Hilton' Is No Trump Hotel," *Politico Magazine*, July 21, 2015. www.politico.com.

at destroying the adversary's culture," writes historian Ruth Seifert. "Because of their cultural position and their important role within the family structure [women] are a principal target if one intends to destroy a culture." Rape used in this way is a form of torture. "Entering a women's body by force has effects that are comparable to torture: It causes physical pain, the loss of personal dignity and self-determination, and it is an attack on the woman's identity,"[12] adds Seifert.

Rape is a common form of torture used by IS fighters in Syria and Iraq to demonstrate their dominance over the people they conquer. A twenty-six-year-old woman identified as Hanan told the organization Human Rights Watch that she was tortured and raped when IS fighters caught her trying to escape from a village they seized in 2016. The IS fighters told Hanan she would have to marry a local IS leader because her husband had fled the oncoming enemy. "Kill me, because I refuse to do that," Hanan told her captors. To force Hanan into submission, the IS members blindfolded her, beat her with plastic cables, and suspended her by her arms. They then removed her blindfold and raped her in front of her children. "The same guy raped me every day for the next month without a blindfold, always in front of my children,"[13] said Hanan.

Although rape has been used by armies as a method of torture throughout history, it was only first recognized as a crime against humanity in 2001. This is when the International Criminal Tribunal for the former Yugoslavia (ICTY) found three veterans of the 1992–1995 Bosnian War guilty of rape, torture, and enslavement of Muslim women in the town of Foca in southeastern Bosnia. "Rape was used by members of the Bosnian Serb armed forces as an instrument of terror," declared Florence Mumba, presiding judge of the ICTY. Addressing the soldiers directly, Mumba added, "You abused and ravaged Muslim women because of their ethnicity and from among their number you picked whomsoever you fancied. You have shown the most glaring disrespect for the women's dignity and their fundamental human rights."[14]

> "Rape was used by members of the Bosnian Serb armed forces as an instrument of terror."[14]
>
> —Florence Mumba, a presiding judge of the International Criminal Tribunal for the former Yugoslavia

Using Torture to Coerce Soldiers

While many wartime activities can be considered torture, the term is generally reserved to describe the practice of inflicting pain to obtain information, force a confession, or coerce soldiers into making propaganda statements. Although torture victims may die during the process, that is not the goal of this kind of torture. Rather, modern torture techniques are designed to inflict the maximum amount of pain *without* putting the victim's life in danger. It is the fear of enduring more pain that generally causes torture victims to break, or give in to the torturer's demands.

During the Vietnam War, for example, US pilots shot down over North Vietnam were routinely tortured until they agreed to confess to war crimes or engage in other propaganda. Sam Johnson, currently a member of the House of Representatives, served as an air force fighter pilot for twenty-nine years. He was shot down over North Vietnam in 1966 and was held as a prisoner of war for seven years. He was beaten, forced to sit on the floor of his cell with his ankles locked between bars known as stocks, and forced to sit for hours on a small stool in an extremely uncomfortable position known as a stress position. After resisting for months, Johnson agreed to sign a false confession that he had committed war crimes against North Vietnam. "You write it and I'll sign it,"[15] Johnson told his captors.

John McCain, a US senator, had a similar experience when serving as a pilot during the Vietnam War. He was shot down over North Vietnam and was tortured until he too signed a confession. "I felt just terrible about it," McCain later wrote. "I kept saying to myself, 'Oh, God, I really didn't have any choice.' I had learned what we all learned over there: Every man has his breaking point. I had reached mine."[16]

Enhanced Interrogation

Countries that have signed international agreements that forbid the torture of POWs like McCain and Johnson are prohibited from engaging in this practice. However, some countries have found ways to get around rules set out in antitorture documents like the 1949 Geneva Conventions, and they torture captives anyway. Consider the various countries fighting terrorist organizations, such as al Qaeda, which perpetrated the September 11, 2001, attacks on the United States. Al Qaeda fighters belong to no specific nation; they fight on behalf of an organization, not a country. Therefore, when such fighters have been captured, they have been called enemy combatants rather than prisoners of war. As a result of this distinction, the US military and the Central Intelligence Agency (CIA) have subjected captives to what they call enhanced interrogation techniques that, according to the Office of Legal Counsel in the Department of Justice, were not necessarily classified as torture. These techniques put the captives under physical and mental duress so that they would provide information, such as the names of other members of the organization, details about their operation, and possible future attacks.

"I had learned what we all learned over there: Every man has his breaking point. I had reached mine."[16]

—John McCain, US senator and former Vietnam War POW

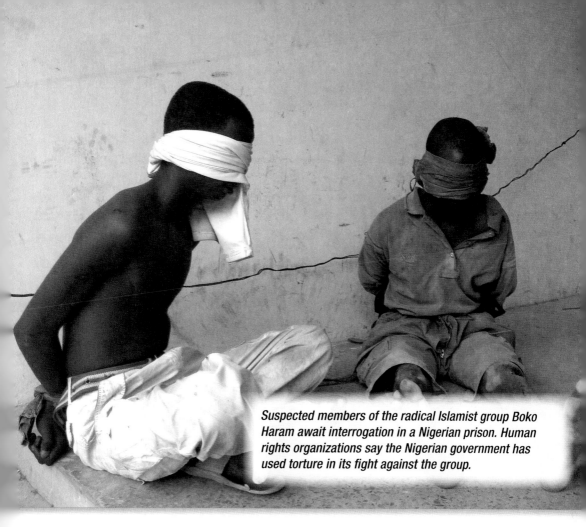

Suspected members of the radical Islamist group Boko Haram await interrogation in a Nigerian prison. Human rights organizations say the Nigerian government has used torture in its fight against the group.

According to a 2014 Senate Intelligence Committee investigation into the interrogations, the physical techniques included depriving the prisoners of sleep for up to 180 hours; sensory deprivation, such as keeping prisoners in total darkness and subjecting them to electronic sounds known as white noise; ice water baths; and waterboarding, a process in which water is poured over a cloth covering a captive's face and breathing passages, which causes a gag reflex and creates the sensation of drowning. Mental enhanced interrogation techniques included mock executions, threats to kill the prisoner, and threats to kill or sexually abuse the prisoner's children and other family members.

"We Crossed a Line"
A report issued by the Senate Intelligence Committee revealed that the techniques used by the CIA were more severe than

previously thought. "Today's release . . . makes crystal clear that the US government used torture,"[17] said Steven W. Hawkins, Amnesty International USA's executive director. Hawkins was not alone in his assessment. Ben Emmerson, a UN official specializing in the protection of human rights, said that US policy allowed the CIA "to commit systematic crimes and gross violations of international human rights law."[18] Even people at the highest levels of government regarded the program as torture. "In the immediate aftermath of 9/11 we did some things that were wrong," said former president Barack Obama of the era of enhanced interrogation techniques. "We did a whole lot of things that were right, but we tortured some folks." He added, "When we engaged in some of these enhanced interrogation techniques, techniques that I believe and I think any fair-minded person would believe were torture, we crossed a line."[19]

Obama ended the enhanced interrogation program, and CIA director John O. Brennan supported the move, saying the program had shortcomings. However, neither Brennan nor his prede-

A First-Person Account of Guantánamo Bay Detention

Mohamedou Ould Slahi, a citizen of Mauritania, was detained at Guantánamo Bay from 2002 to 2016. He wrote an account of his confinement, portions of which were published by *Slate* magazine in 2013:

In the block the recipe started. I was deprived of my comfort items, except for a thin iso-mat and a very thin, small, and worn-out blanket. I was deprived of my books, which I owned. I was deprived of my Quran. I was deprived of my soap. I was deprived of my toothpaste. I was deprived of the roll of toilet paper I had. The cell—better, the box—was cooled down so that I was shaking most of the time. I was forbidden from seeing the light of the day. Every once in a while they gave me a rec time in the night to keep me from seeing or interacting with any detainees. I was living literally in terror. I don't remember having slept one night quietly; for the next 70 days to come I wouldn't know the sweetness of sleeping. Interrogation for 24 hours, three and sometimes four shifts a day. I rarely got a day off.

Mohamedou Ould Slahi, "The Guantánamo Memoirs of Mohamedou Ould Slahi," *Slate*, May 2, 2013. www.slate.com.

cessors, who oversaw the program, believe it rose to the level of torture. Former CIA directors George Tenet, Porter Goss, and Michael V. Hayden criticized the findings of the Senate Intelligence Committee report, calling it "a partisan attack on the agency that has done the most to protect America after the 9/11 attacks."[20] Former vice president Dick Cheney, who supported enhanced interrogation when he served with the George W. Bush administration, was even blunter. "What I keep hearing out there is they portray this as a rogue operation and the agency was way out of bounds and then they lied about it," he told the *New York Times* in 2014. "I think that's all a bunch of hooey. The program was authorized. The agency did not want to proceed without authorization, and it was also reviewed legally by the Justice Department before they undertook the program." Cheney rejected the description of the interrogation techniques as "torture," adding that the program was "the right thing to do, and if I had to do it over again, I would do it."[21]

> "In the immediate aftermath of 9/11 we did some things that were wrong. We did a whole lot of things that were right, but we tortured some folks."[19]
>
> —Barack Obama, former president of the United States

The Prevalence of Torture

Both enhanced interrogation techniques and more blatant forms of torture are usually conducted in secret, making it difficult to know how many people are affected. For example, the CIA moved some of the people they were interrogating to nations such as Poland, Lithuania, or Romania, which do not have strict antitorture policies. This practice is known as rendition, and it makes it very difficult to know how many people are involved.

Although the exact number of torture victims is unknown, Amnesty International reports that torture is currently practiced in at least 122 nations. Some of these countries, such as Afghanistan, Iraq, Libya, Pakistan, and Yemen, are involved in armed conflicts with other nations, and most of the torture is related to obtaining military secrets. Other countries, such as Burundi, Somalia, South Sudan, Cameroon, the Central African Republic, and Nigeria, are embroiled in civil wars or violent public unrest. In these cases, torture is often used to learn the identities of members or supporters of

Two Mexican federal police officers lie dead near their crashed truck after an attack. The Mexican government has been accused of torturing people suspected in violent attacks on federal police.

antigovernment groups or to punish them for their activities. Some countries, such as Mexico and Honduras, are fighting drug cartels. Government forces may torture suspects to gain information about the cartels or as retribution for violence committed against police officers. Many other countries, including Israel and the United States, are fighting terrorists and sometimes torture them in hopes of gaining information about their members and operations. "Torture is banned, but in two-thirds of the world's countries it is still being committed in secret," says Amnesty International's Peter Benenson. "Too many governments still allow wrongful imprisonment, murder, or 'disappearance' with impunity."[22]

Who Are the Torturers?

Military, intelligence, and police forces are responsible for much of the world's torture, but others practice torture as well. These can include sadists (people who derive pleasure from the pain of others), sexual abusers, and hate crime perpetrators. For example, in 1987 Philadelphia police responding to a 911 call found three women chained to a sewer pipe in the basement of the home of a wealthy stock investor named Gary Heidnik. A fourth woman, Josefina Rivera, had managed to escape and called the police. According to the survivors, Heidnik raped and tortured the women while the others were forced to watch. He eventually killed two of his six victims. His motive was nothing more than sadistic pleasure. The Heidnik case was one of the inspirations behind the Buffalo Bill character in Thomas Harris's book *The Silence of the Lambs*.

Criminal organizations also use torture to punish enemies, obtain information, and force people to cooperate with them. Drug cartels from Afghanistan, Colombia, Mexico, China, Thailand, and Russia all use torture to inspire fear among competitors, law enforcement, and members of their communities. For example, in 2016 a woman in her twenties was tortured and murdered by members of a drug cartel as a warning to people not to cooperate with Gilberto "El Chanda" Gómez Romero, leader of the Los H3, or Third Brotherhood, drug cartel. The victim's body was left in the streets of Apatzingan, Mexico, with a message warning others not to support Romero.

Governments also practice torture outside of wartime contexts. For example, in countries such as North Korea, Iran, Syria, Honduras, and China, where there is limited journalistic freedom and freedom of movement, the government practices torture without fearing criticism by their own people or condemnation abroad. For example, in 2017 Afsana Byazidi, a Kurdish student activist serving a four-year jail term in Iran, smuggled a letter to human rights organizations in which she reported being raped and tortured while being interrogated at an Iranian intelligence detention center. Addressing the letter to Iran's supreme leader, Ali Khamenei, Byazidi wrote, "I will not forget the imprisonment, torture and rape that I and others were subjected to. There will come a day when we will hold you and your allies accountable."[23]

From soldiers and enemy combatants to political activists and victims of drug wars, men and women around the world are being tortured for a wide range of reasons. Some, like the CIA detainees, are being tortured to obtain information that authorities believe may help prevent a terrorist attack. Others, like Byazidi, are being punished for speaking out against the government. Still others, like Abdel Razzaq Jalal, are being tortured so they will not resist invading forces. Some, like Hanan in Iraq and the Muslim women in the town of Foca in Bosnia, were tortured because of their religious faith. Still others, like Josefina Rivera, who was tortured by a sadist in Philadelphia, and the young Mexican woman tortured by members of a drug cartel in Apatzingan, Mexico, were simply in the wrong place at the wrong time.

Whatever the reason, torture is never permitted under international law, but human rights activists say that nations are not doing enough to stop it. "Torturers are able to do the despicable things . . . and get away with it, not because they are lone wolves, but because they are supported and protected often by a cast of hundreds . . . and the same thing applies at the governmental level," says Secretary-General Alex Neve of Amnesty International Canada. "Governments are able to preside over and allow extensive torture in their countries because they are supported and protected by other governments."[24]

Chapter 2

What Constitutes Torture?

Focus Questions

1. What is the main difference between torture and other forms of human brutality?

2. Is mental abuse a form of torture? Why or why not?

3. In your opinion, who should decide whether an act is torture? The victim? The person performing the act? Or someone else?

Torture has a widely accepted definition of physical abuse designed to control another person's actions. However, examples of torture vary widely from person to person. Some people think of medieval torture machines such as the rack, which stretched a victim's limbs to and beyond the breaking point. Others think of more modern methods, such as forcing the victim to stand for many hours or to sit in a confined stress position. Still others think of enhanced interrogation techniques, such as waterboarding. Is it torture to force a prisoner to listen to loud music? Is verbal abuse torture? Defining what torture is—and what it is not—is an important legal and societal issue.

In 2014 Amnesty International catalogued twenty-seven methods of torture that had been used on victims worldwide during the previous year. "Common torture methods included beatings, electric shocks, sleep deprivation, stress positions, prolonged suspension by the wrists or ankles and threats against detainees and their loved ones."[25] Some types of torture were employed systematically, on multiple victims. Others were limited to a single incident. It is possible that new forms of torture were introduced that ended up killing the victim and therefore went unnoticed and unreported. Because torture is conducted in secret, it is impossible to know everything that is being done.

The UN Definition of Torture

In 1948, after the widespread abuses of civilians and prisoners of war during World War II, the UN General Assembly included a prohibition against torture in its Universal Declaration of Human Rights. Article 5 of the agreement states, "No one shall be subjected to torture or to cruel, inhuman or degrading treatment or punishment." The UN later defined what it meant by torture on December 10, 1984, when it adopted an agreement known as the Convention Against Torture and Other Inhuman or Degrading Treatment or Punishment. This document defined torture as "any act by which severe pain or suffering, whether physical or mental, is intentionally inflicted on a person for such purposes as obtaining from him, or a third person, information or a confession, punishing him for an act he or a third person has committed or is suspected of having committed, or intimidating or coercing him."[26] Since it took effect in 1987, the agreement has been ratified by 161 nations and serves as the international standard for defining torture.

Although the convention provides a good definition of torture, critics of the agreement say it is confusing because it makes exceptions for pain caused in the normal course of enforcing a country's laws or carrying out justice. Most countries agree, for example, that pain arising from capital punishment (also called the death penalty), which is legal in the United States, China, and other countries, is not torture, because it is a lawful punishment and the purpose of the punishment is not pain, but death. However, some death penalty critics disagree. They say that condemned prisoners often feel extreme pain for a prolonged period, especially when they are killed using a combination of drugs administered by intravenous infusions, known as lethal injections. For example, the 2014 execution of Joseph Ru-

> "Common torture methods included beatings, electric shocks, sleep deprivation, stress positions, prolonged suspension by the wrists or ankles and threats against detainees and their loved ones."[25]
>
> —Amnesty International, a human rights organization

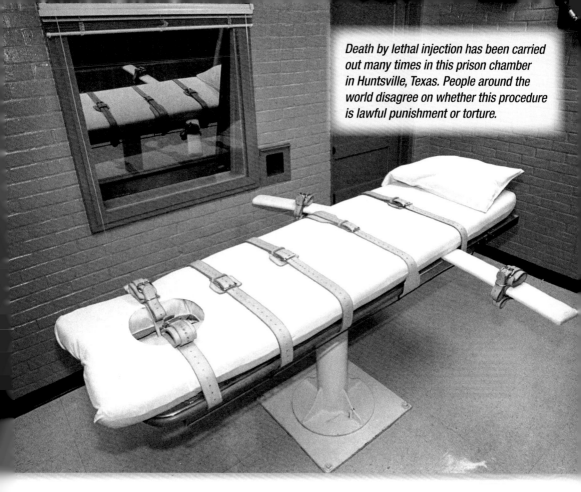

Death by lethal injection has been carried out many times in this prison chamber in Huntsville, Texas. People around the world disagree on whether this procedure is lawful punishment or torture.

dolph Wood III in Arizona lasted for nearly two hours. According to Michael Kiefer, a reporter who witnessed the execution, Wood gasped 660 times before he died. In addition, one of these drugs has the effect of making the prisoner unable to move or speak. As a result, it is impossible for witnesses to tell how much pain the prisoner is in. Because pain that occurs during lawful activities like the death penalty is not considered torture under the convention, many human rights activists see the agreement as a loophole for countries to conduct torture.

Black Torture

Some actions are more readily recognized as torture than others. These clear-cut acts of torture are sometimes referred to as black torture. Extreme examples include breaking bones, such as the fractured shinbones found in the mass grave of Schöneck-Kilianstädten. Black torture can also include administering painful electrical shocks. This happened to a man named Adam, one of

Sexual Torture in Spain

A young Basque woman identified only as victim ILMW03 described the sexual abuse she suffered while being questioned by Spanish authorities for being a possible member of the Basque separatist group Euskadi Ta Askatasuna:

> One of [the police officers] playing the role of an oversexed pervert or so (aside from being a role there must have been some truth in it because it is difficult to play that role so well for five days), and he commented that he had had his weekend screwed (it was Thursday), but it was okay because he was going to take advantage of me, and he ended up saying that he was going to rape me. That threat was made from the beginning and he then started touching me. I could not do anything; I was handcuffed behind my back and I was between two policemen and with my head down. I tried to put my shoulder in between to stop him touching me, but I was completely helpless. That he touched me was disgusting. . . . He made comments like: "If you think about having kids forget it, because after going through our hands you will not be able to. . . ." When they touched me, they said things like: "Oh, you're too skinny! Well, you're going to see, because I do not like skinny girls. . . ." Degrading treatment, it was very humiliating and degrading.

Quoted in Istanbul Protocol Project in the Basque Country Working Group, *Incommunicado Detention and Torture in Spain*, 2016, p. 95. http://tbinternet.ohchr.org.

many gay men rounded up by police in the Russian republic of Chechnya as part of a campaign against homosexuality in 2017. Adam told the *Guardian* newspaper that his captors attached metal clamps to his fingers and toes and then cranked the handle of a crude electric generator, sending powerful jolts of electricity through his body. "Sometimes they were trying to get information from me; other times they were just amusing themselves,"[27] he said. Adam is not the only gay man who was tortured in this way. "We are talking about the mass persecution of gay people, with hundreds of people kidnapped by authorities," said Igor Kochetkov, a gay rights activist in St. Petersburg, Russia. "This is unprecedented not only in Russia but in recent world history. There is little doubt that we are dealing with crimes against humanity."[28]

Black torture also can include other heinous acts, such as the amputations of ears, fingers, toes, and even limbs. The most common form of torture is to beat a victim with hands, whips, rubber hoses, rods, or other implements. This is what happened to Cihad Saatcioglu. After a failed coup attempt in Turkey in 2016, thousands of opponents of the government were rounded up and tortured, including Saatcioglu. "From the moment I was detained until I was brought to hospital I was constantly beaten," Saatcioglu recalls. "It was endless—slapping, kicking, banging our heads against the wall." The torture was not conducted by "lone wolves," acting on their own, according to Saatcioglu. "If it was only a few officers, you might think it was an exception. But it was the motorcycle police, plain-clothes ones, anti-terror—they were all there. They were confident while torturing us."[29]

Black torture also includes applying extreme heat to the body via burning cigarettes, heated metal, or hot liquids such as wax, plastic, oil, or water. Piercing the body, especially slowly, is a common form of torture. This can include stabbing, puncturing with needles, and having metal or bamboo forced under the fingernails. A thirty-one-year-old Syrian man told Human Rights Watch how intelligence agents of the Syrian government tortured him in the Idlib Central Prison: "They forced me to undress. Then they started squeezing my fingers with pliers. They put staples in my

A general and others who took part in a coup attempt in 2016 are brought to court by armed Turkish soldiers. Thousands of people have been arrested and tortured in connection with the coup attempt.

fingers, chest, and ears. I was only allowed to take them out if I spoke. The nails in the ears were the most painful."[30]

Some torture involves placing a person in a so-called stress position. This can be accomplished by forcing the victim to sit or stand in a confined space and not allowing them to change position. Mohamedou Ould Slahi, a former prisoner at the American detention facility at Guantánamo Bay, Cuba, described a stress position used during his interrogation:

> When I failed to give [the interrogator] the answer he wanted to hear, he made me stand up, with my back bent because my hands were shackled with my feet and waist and locked to the floor. [The interrogator] . . . made sure that the guards maintained me in that situation until he decided otherwise. He . . . kept me hurt during his lunch, which took at least two to three hours.[31]

Although stress positions are not violent and rarely leave marks on the body, they can cause excruciating pain.

Torture in Mexico

In a report on the torture of women in Mexico, Amnesty International tells the story of Mónica Esparza Castro, who was stopped by police along with her brother and husband:

> The officers showed no warrant, but took the three to a warehouse behind the offices of the Municipal Security Department in Torreón. According to Monica, when she entered [an official] said to her "welcome to the party" and she saw her brother and husband sitting naked with blood streaming down their bodies. The police officers grabbed Mónica and began to simulate drowning by plunging her head into a bucket on repeated occasions. They then suffocated her with plastic bags, beat her buttocks with a wooden board, and dragged her along the floor by her hair. They continued to ask her questions that Mónica could not answer. . . . After more than twelve hours in police custody, Mónica . . . was forced to sign a "confession" saying she was part of the Zeta drug cartel.

Amnesty International, *Surviving Death: Police and Military Torture of Women in Mexico*. London: Amnesty International, 2016, p. 20.

Intimate Violations

Sexual abuse, such as rape (including rape with foreign objects), is a form of torture. By gaining control over the victim's body and violating it, the torturer not only terrifies and hurts the victim but also wreaks mental damage. Describing the use of rape during the Algerian War (1954–1962), historian Joshua Cole writes, "Torture and rape were about establishing a particular relationship between French soldiers and Algerian Muslims, one in which the most essential parts of a victim's personality—the integrity of their bodies, their relations with their families, their connection to a religion, a cause—were annihilated."[32]

This form of torture continues to be used. Consider what a young Basque woman—identified only as victim JZLV03—told the Istanbul Protocol Project in the Basque Country Working Group, an affiliation of several human rights organizations studying interrogation techniques in the Basque region of northern Spain. In 2016 she described how she was raped by Spanish authorities who were interrogating her for being a suspected member of the armed Basque separatist group Euskadi Ta Askatasuna, meaning "Basque Homeland and Liberty"). "At one point they stripped me and began to poke some fingers through my anus, they told me that they were going to poke in a stick," she reported. "I was there with my eyes closed, crying. It was like a nightmare, I could not control anything. It was a feeling that I was lost and they could do whatever they wanted with me."[33]

> "I was there with my eyes closed, crying. It was like a nightmare, I could not control anything. It was a feeling that I was lost and they could do whatever they wanted with me."[33]
>
> —A female Basque torture victim identified as JZLV03

Women are not the only ones subjected to this kind of torture. Kamil Uluc, another person rounded up after the failed coup in Turkey in 2016, says that Turkish authorities attempted to rape him with a foreign object. "They took me to a dark room and tried to forcefully insert a baton into my anus," Uluc recounts. "When they couldn't do it, they left. Maybe I will forget the other torture—but for the sexual part, it is carved into the dirtiest corner of my heart."[34] According to the 2014 Senate Intelligence Committee report on torture after the 9/11 attacks, several detainees in Guantánamo Bay were force-fed and hydrated through the rectum. Although the food and water were administered to maintain the health of the detainees— who were resisting eating and drinking—nevertheless, the forced nature of the feeding was deemed severe and humiliating enough to be considered rape. "It's aggravated sexual assault, there's no question about it," says Wells Dixon, an attorney for Majid Khan, one of the force-fed detainees. "It's forcible rape."[35] Other unwanted medical interventions, such as being forced to take drugs, have an abortion, or be sterilized, are also considered forms of black torture.

White Torture

While black torture can be an effective way of making a torture victim break, sometimes the bodily harm is so great that the victim loses consciousness or is in too much pain to provide the torturers with any information or comply with their demands. As a result, torturers have developed techniques that scare or otherwise intimidate a person without causing the same level of physical damage as black torture. This kind of torture is known as white torture.

Some white torture techniques are directed at the mind more than at the body. For example, some white torture victims might be threatened with violence aimed at them or their family. Uluc says he was threatened in this way by Turkish officers. "'If you don't speak, we'll bring your wife here and rape her in front of your eyes,'"[36] Uluc recalls. The same technique is used throughout the world. "They said that they would take me to prison, that my parents would not be allowed to open their business, that they would grab and rape my girlfriend," said a young Basque man, describing techniques used on him by Spanish authorities. "That really affected me, though I tried to show them that it did not."[37] Sometimes these threats are made while the victim is forced to watch or listen to others being tortured or raped.

Mock executions are another form of white torture. During these sessions, the victim is made to believe that he or she is about to be executed. Mock executions seem completely real until the executioner's weapon fails to discharge. Such sessions can produce tremendous fear and psychological pain. Daniel Keller, a US Army soldier who served as a prison guard during the Iraq War, later said that he and other the soldiers sometimes staged mock executions. Keller said they would pull an Iraqi out of jail to, say, go to the bathroom. Once outside, someone would discharge a gun, and the Iraqis in the jail would think the prisoner had been killed. "They would be crying whenever we came in to take someone to go to the bathroom because they thought they were about to be executed,"[38] said Keller.

Some white torture involves powerful sensory abuse. For example, victims of white torture might be exposed to loud music, bright lights, and intense questioning for long periods of time. Others might be subjected to the odor of feces, urine, or chemicals. Many are deprived of sleep, which can cause auditory and visual hallucinations and greatly affect the body's normal functioning. Some victims are humiliated by being made to remove their clothing in front of others. For example, at the Abu Ghraib prison,

A 2003 photograph from Iraq's Abu Ghraib prison shows an unidentified detainee standing on a box with a bag over his head and wires attached to him. Humiliation and degrading poses are considered a form of torture.

a facility shared by the Iraqi government and the American forces that invaded Iraq in 2003, male detainees were made to get undressed in front of both male and female American soldiers and pose in degrading positions to be photographed.

Subjecting prisoners to extreme temperatures is another way to make them so uncomfortable that they might be tempted to give up information to get out of the situation. "The consequences of the cold room are devastating," remembers former Guantánamo Bay detainee Slahi.

> The interrogators turned the AC all the way down trying to reach 0 [degrees] F, but obviously the AC is not designed to kill. . . . The AC fought its way to 49 F, and if you are interested in math like me, that is 9.4 C—in other words very, very cold, especially for somebody who had to stay in it more than 12 hours, had no underwear, had a very thin uniform, and comes from a hot country.[39]

Cruel, Inhuman, and Degrading (CID) Treatment

Other cruel, inhuman, or degrading (CID) treatment is not necessarily classified as torture, but it still draws concern from human rights activists. Even though CID treatment is not as severe as torture, it still is prohibited by the UN Convention Against Torture. "Examples of such prohibited mistreatment include being forced to stand spread eagled against the wall; being subjected to bright lights or blindfolding; being subjected to continuous loud noise; being deprived of sleep, food or drink; being subjected to forced constant standing or crouching; or violent shaking," states Human Rights Watch. "In essence, any form of physical treatment used to intimidate, coerce or 'break' a person during an interrogation constitutes prohibited ill-treatment."[40]

The difference between CID treatment and torture often is a matter of how intense the mistreatment is, how long it lasts, and whether other kinds of mistreatment are

"In essence, any form of physical treatment used to intimidate, coerce or 'break' a person during an interrogation constitutes prohibited ill-treatment."[40]

—Human Rights Watch, a nonprofit organization devoted to defending human rights also inflicted at the same time. For example, forcing a prisoner to stand spread-eagled against the wall for an hour might be considered mistreatment, but keeping a person in that position for several hours would constitute torture. Similarly, keeping a detainee blindfolded for hours while being moved from one facility to another for security reasons might be mistreatment, but keeping the prisoner blindfolded for several days would be torture. "If these practices are intense enough, prolonged in duration, or combined with other measures that result in severe pain or suffering, they can qualify as torture,"[41] states Human Rights Watch.

Like torture, mistreatment depends on the reason the person inflicts the pain or discomfort. For example, police officers often handle suspects in a rough manner when making an arrest, especially if the suspects do not follow directions or resist arrest. If the treatment is intended to degrade the person or to elicit information, it might be considered CID treatment. However, if the officer only seeks to subdue the person, it would not necessarily be considered mistreatment. Since the enforcement of laws is a legal endeavor, most law enforcement actions would be shielded by the UN convention's clause that provides exceptions for pain or suffering arising from lawful actions.

Chapter 3

Is Torture Ever Justified?

Focus Questions

1. Is information obtained through torture reliable? Explain your answer.

2. Is saving a single life a valid reason to torture? In your opinion, how many lives would have to be saved to justify torture? Explain your reasoning.

3. Some people say the use of torture makes society safer. Others say it puts society at greater risk. Which do you think is the case? Why?

Torture is so abhorrent that the laws prohibiting it are sometimes said to belong to a category of law above all others, known as *jus cogens*—a Latin phrase meaning "compelling law." *Jus cogens* laws reflect a norm accepted by all people in all situations. They are so basic to civilization that they supersede all other laws and treaties. For example, laws against genocide and slavery are considered *jus cogens* because no civilized person defends those practices. Human rights organizations believe that laws against torture belong in this category.

While the vast majority of people condemn the use of torture, however, not everyone agrees that it should never be used. They argue that in certain situations, torture is justified. Most agree that torture should never be used as a punishment for any crime, no matter how terrible the crime. The Eighth Amendment of the US Constitution expressly prohibits "cruel and unusual punishment," which by definition includes torture. Antonin Scalia, a Supreme

Court justice from 1986 until his death in 2016, agreed that the Eighth Amendment prohibits torture as a punishment, but he told an audience at a Swiss university in 2014 that the Constitution goes no further than that. "The Constitution itself says nothing about torture," he said. "The Constitution speaks of punishment. If you condemn someone who has committed a crime to torture, that would be unconstitutional."[42]

The Ticking Time Bomb Scenario

Scalia suggested that the Constitution would not prohibit torturing someone to obtain information in an extreme life-or-death situation. "I think it's very facile [naive] for people to say, 'Oh, torture is terrible,'" said Scalia. "You posit the situation where a person that you know for sure knows the location of a nuclear bomb that has been planted in Los Angeles and will kill millions of people. You think it's an easy question? You think it's clear that you cannot use extreme measures to get that information out of that person?"[43]

The situation Scalia described is often called the ticking time bomb scenario. Jeff McMahan, a philosophy professor at the University of Oxford, summarizes the idea behind the ticking time bomb scenario by describing it in the context of a decision sometimes faced by law enforcement: whether to kill one person in order to save many. "It can be morally justifiable to kill a person to prevent him from detonating a bomb that will kill innocent people, or to prevent him from killing an innocent hostage," he writes. "Since being killed is generally worse than being tortured, it should therefore be justifiable to torture a person to prevent him from killing innocent people." McMahan further justifies the use of torture in such a scenario by saying that the torture could actually be avoided if the person with information decided to cooperate. "In cases in which torture is defensive in this way, the person tortured is not wronged," he argues. "Indeed, he could avoid the torture simply by doing what he is morally required to do anyway—namely, disclose the location of the bomb or hostage."[44]

> "Since being killed is generally worse than being tortured, it should therefore be justifiable to torture a person to prevent him from killing innocent people."[44]
>
> —Jeff McMahan, a professor of philosophy at the University of Oxford

31

Human rights groups say torture is never justified. Supreme Court justice Antonin Scalia (pictured in 2014) had a more nuanced view of this issue, suggesting that torture might be acceptable in extreme life-or-death situations.

McMahan and Scalia are not the only ones to suggest that torture might be acceptable in certain cases. Alan Dershowitz, a well-known legal scholar, argued in his 2002 book, *Why Terrorism Works: Understanding the Threat, Responding to the Challenge,* that there are times when it is appropriate to use torture. In fact, Dershowitz says the issue "is not whether some torture would or would not be used in the ticking-bomb case—it would. The question is whether it would be done openly, pursuant to a previously established legal procedure, or whether it would be done secretly, in violation of existing law."[45]

Problems with the Time Bomb Premise

Others are not so sure that torture would be appropriate even in a ticking time bomb scenario. Most critics of the ticking time bomb scenario do not dispute the logic of making the preservation of human life more important than taking a moral stand against torture. Instead, they criticize the premise of the scenario, pointing out that it assumes many factors that most likely would never be present or, possibly, could never be known. As a result, the premise leads to false and possibly dangerous conclusions.

For example, the scenario presumes that authorities know an attack is imminent but do not know when or where the attack will take place. It further assumes that authorities have in custody a person who they are certain can supply the missing information. If that person refuses to cooperate and the authorities decide to torture him, the torture would have to succeed quickly—not only before the bomb goes off but also with enough time for the authorities to find the bomb or evacuate the area where it will occur. Getting the person to talk would not be easy, even if they were tortured; anyone involved in such a plot would likely be willing to die rather than give up information. Forms of white torture that might cause the person to break over a long period of time would be useless because time would run out before the information could be obtained.

Fighting Fire with Fire

In 2007, *Washington Post* reporter Laura Blumenfeld interviewed a man identified only as James about interrogation techniques he used when he worked for the Special Branch of Northern Ireland's Royal Ulster Constabulary during the 1970s. At the time, Irish nationalists were conducting a terror campaign designed to drive the British out of Northern Ireland. Around eighteen hundred people died during the armed campaign, including about eleven hundred members of the British security forces and about 640 civilians. James interrogated many suspected terrorists using harsh methods. For example, he once placed a loaded gun to the head of Brendan Hughes, the leader of the Irish Republican Army, an armed Irish separatist group, and threatened his life. James believes such tactics were completely justified:

> You fight fire with fire. If it's going to save lives, you're entitled to use whatever means you can. . . .

> You've got to get up and get on with it—that's what we did. . . . Yes, a bloke [guy] would get a cuff in the ear or he might brace against the wall. Yes, they had sleep deprivation. . . . But we did not torture.

> My friend once saw a guy planting a bomb. My friend tied a rope around the guy's ankle, and made him defuse it. Now that's how to deal with a ticking bomb.

Quoted in Laura Blumenfeld, "The Tortured Lives of Interrogators," *Washington Post*, June 4, 2007. www.washingtonpost .com.

Most important, the authorities would need to be able to determine whether the information the person gives under torture is true. Critics of the scenario point out that simply by lying, the torture victim can stop the torture but also ensure the success of the plot because the authorities would waste valuable time checking the wrong location, or locations, until time runs out.

Critics of the ticking time bomb scenario argue that to make an ethical choice to torture, the torturer must know or be reasonably sure that the torture will produce the desired result. However, in a real-life situation, it would be impossible for the torturer to predict ahead of time whether the torture will succeed. Torturers cannot know for certain whether the person in their custody possesses the information they want, whether he or she will divulge the information within the allotted time, or whether the information will be accurate. Since the outcome of the torture is unknowable ahead of time, critics contend that the torturer is not making a true choice, balancing one known value against another.

Even if torture is successful in a ticking time bomb scenario, the torturer might not know all the consequences of the act until much later, if at all. It is possible that the torture will launch a downward spiral of violence that would cost more lives than the original torture saved. Critics argue that using torture, or setting a policy that torture will be used, is a slippery slope: once you start down it, it is hard to go back. It will make it easier to torture people and will make enemies more likely to use torture as well. This will lead to increased violence, more victims, and a never-ending cycle of retaliation. According to this view, the torturer cannot know all of the consequences of the torture and, therefore, cannot make an informed decision about whether or not it is moral.

Antitorture Absolutism

Some people reject the use of torture in any scenario. They point out that Article 2.2 of the UN's Convention Against Torture explicitly forbids any exceptions to the prohibition against torture.

It states, "No exceptional circumstances whatsoever, whether a state of war or a threat of war, internal instability or any other public emergency, may be invoked as a justification for torture."[46] Antitorture advocates say that since people will be tempted to torture in the ticking time bomb and other scenarios, only an absolute ban on torture can prevent the kind of futile torture that will occur because of the torturer's misplaced confidence.

Torturing Prisoners of War

The logic of using torture to save lives also applies during times of war. For example, the capture of an enemy soldier can be similar to the ticking time bomb scenario because the captive might have information about troop movements and war plans that could save hundreds, even thousands of lives. However, the same problems that plague the ticking time bomb scenario apply to the case of the POW, especially the difficulty of knowing ahead

An American prisoner of war talks to a fellow prisoner through a barred opening at a North Vietnamese detention camp in 1973. Although the Geneva Convention prohibits torture, North Vietnam ignored this international agreement.

of time if the captured soldier possesses any lifesaving information. In addition, the torture victim could provide false information that could do more harm than good, causing forces to be sent to the wrong locations. Perhaps the strongest argument against torturing a POW is that it invites the enemy to torture as well.

For these and other reasons, the Geneva Conventions place an absolute ban on the torture and mistreatment of POWs. Article 3 of the Third Geneva Convention states,

> Persons taking no active part in the hostilities, including members of armed forces who have laid down their arms . . . shall in all circumstances be treated humanely, without any adverse distinction founded on race, color, religion or faith, sex, birth or wealth, or any other similar criteria. To this end the following acts are and shall remain prohibited at any time and in any place whatsoever with respect to the above-mentioned persons:
>
> (a) violence to life and person, in particular murder of all kinds, mutilation, cruel treatment and torture; . . .
>
> (c) outrages upon personal dignity, in particular, humiliating and degrading treatment.[47]

Article 17 expressly forbids the use of torture to obtain information during wartime. It states that "no physical or mental torture, nor any other form of coercion, may be inflicted on prisoners of war to secure from them information of any kind whatever."[48]

While the prohibitions of torture in the Geneva Conventions leave little room for confusion, questions arise when one side fighting a war does not follow the international agreements. During the Vietnam War, for example, North Vietnam ignored the Geneva Conventions, torturing American captives such as Sam Johnson and John McCain. Some people believe that torture is justified when used against enemies who do not adhere to the Geneva Conventions and other human rights agreements. "This new paradigm [the war on terrorism] renders obsolete Geneva's strict limitations on questioning of enemy prisoners and renders quaint some of its provisions,"[49] wrote White House counsel Alberto Gonzales in a 2004 memo. The belief that it is dangerous for a country to follow the rules of warfare if the other side does not is exactly the kind of slippery slope that human rights advocates warn about. They say that engaging in torture starts a downward spiral that puts a nation's soldiers at risk for being tortured if they are captured. Former CIA chief Stansfield Turner supports this view. In 2004 Turner said that ignoring the Geneva Conventions and other international agreements "makes US citizens, especially military personnel, more vulnerable to similar treatment."[50]

A Propaganda Aid

Another argument against using torture is that when the public learns about the mistreatment, the country's reputation will be damaged. In turn, such acts can be used as a powerful propaganda tool for the other side. They might use pictures or stories of the torture victims to inspire more people to fight. "Violations of the Geneva Convention can turn a people against the United States and toward the guerrillas or terrorists," says Ivan Eland, an analyst with the Independent Institute in Oakland, California. "It can also act as a recruiting tool for terrorists."[51] Former presi-

Some experts say that stories and images of torture have been used as a recruitment tool by extremist groups such as the Taliban (pictured) in Afghanistan.

dent George W. Bush wrote in his memoir, *Decision Points,* that placing enemy combatants in the Guantánamo Bay detention center ended up damaging the United States in this way. "The detention facility had become a propaganda tool for our enemies and a distraction for our allies,"[52] Bush explained. An example of this kind of propaganda appeared in the spring 2014 issue of *Inspire,* an al Qaeda publication in the Arabian Peninsula. Al Qaeda propagandist Abu Abdillāh Amoravid wrote,

We are certain that the sweet dream America propagated vanished into a terrifying nightmare: Abu Ghraib, black sites, Guantanamo and the US soldiers' crimes in Afghanistan and Iraq are too clear to need clarification. Actually, there is no possible way to express these inhumane crimes perpetrated against human rights. Here we could say America has lost the most important element of global leadership: morals and principles.[53]

Popular Support for Torture

Despite the drawbacks, some public opinion polls have found that an increasing number of Americans support the use of torture in certain circumstances. For example, a 2016 poll taken by the International Committee of the Red Cross found that 46 percent of Americans support torturing enemy combatants. This is a dramatic, nineteen-point increase in the support of torture from a similar poll taken ten years earlier by Rasmussen Reports, an American polling company. In October 2007 the Rasmussen survey found that only 27 percent of Americans thought the United States should torture prisoners captured in the fight against terrorism. Even more striking, the number of Americans opposed to torture dropped from 65 percent in the Red Cross's 1999 poll to just 30 percent in the organization's 2016 poll, a decline of thirty-five points.

A POW Gives Misleading Information

Torturing prisoners of war can backfire on the torturers when victims provide unreliable information or even deliberate misinformation. This is what happened when Marcus McDilda, an American fighter pilot, was shot down over Japanese territory during World War II. McDilda was captured and tortured after the first atomic bombs were used on the Japanese cities of Hiroshima and Nagasaki. The Japanese wanted to get information about the devastating new weapons. Until the bombs were used, their existence had been top secret, so McDilda knew nothing about them. However, McDilda decided to intentionally mislead his torturers, telling them that the United States had one hundred more nuclear weapons and planned to use them on Tokyo over the next several days. Word of the confession was passed through military channels to the Japanese war minister, who informed the cabinet. Based on the grim but false information, the Japanese decided to surrender.

Polls like these suggest that as long as people believe torture will save lives, they will continue to find its use justified. Very few people would describe themselves as torture advocates, but many agree with a man identified only by his code name, Sheriff. The former chief of interrogations for Shin Bet, Israel's security service, Sheriff used to interrogate captured terrorists. "You have to play by different rules," Sheriff told the *Washington Post*. "The terrorists want to use your own system to destroy you."[54]

The Consequences of Torture

Torturers usually offer their victims a sort of bargain—that the pain will stop as soon as the victim gives in to the torturer's demands. The bargain is often accepted, but it is not always kept, because the physical and mental effects of torture can last long after the torture is over. The long-term effects of torture can have serious consequences for victims, their families, and even the torturers themselves.

The physical effects of torture are usually temporary. Pain from electric shocks, simulated drowning, stress positions, and intense pressure placed on parts of the body normally subside after the torture ceases. Bruises from beatings or from being tightly bound normally disappear after a few weeks. However, the physical effects of some kinds of torture can be permanent.

Long-Term Physical Effects

Cuts, burns, and lesions from whipping can leave scars. Being suspended by the ankles or wrists can cause permanent damage to joints. Broken bones often fail to mend properly, especially when the torture victim is not given adequate medical attention. For example, John McCain is unable to raise his hand above his head because his arm, which was broken when he was tortured as a prisoner of war during the Vietnam War, was never properly treated during the five and a half years that he was held in captivity.

Arizona Senator and former US Navy pilot John McCain, photographed with his squadron in 1965, was shot down over Vietnam in 1967. McCain still has physical problems stemming from torture during his years as a prisoner of war.

Even prolonged exposure to bright light can cause permanent damage. Said Abaceen, a suspected terrorist detained at Bagram Air Base, the largest US military base in Afghanistan, in 2003, said that when prisoners broke the rules, such as not to speak with one another, they were forced to stare into a bright light. "It was not only me," said Abaceen. "I think all the prisoners there were speaking to each other and [were forced] to look into the light, [for] one night or for [about] ten hours."[55] Abaceen later learned that his eyes had sustained permanent damage. He now has to always wear sunglasses to lessen the pain.

Sometimes torture leads to permanent medical conditions, such as limb loss, vision or hearing loss, respiratory problems, other long-term disabilities, and even death. For example, in April 2017 an eleven-year-old boy named Mohamad Thaqif Amin Mohd Gadaffi was beaten on his lower legs with a water hose by his school warden in Kota Tinggi, Malaysia. Gadaffi developed blood clots in his legs that caused a bacterial infection to spread to other parts of his body. "The legs had to be amputated to prevent any further damage to his worsening condition," said Datuk Ayub Rahmat, a health official with the Malaysian government. The amputation did not stop the infection, and the boy died four days later. According to a video obtained by police, Gadaffi was not the school official's only victim. "In the recording, the warden was seen whipping about 15 students,"[56] said Kota Tinggi police chief Rahmat Othman. The beatings occurred on multiple occasions—not to punish the students for something they had done but rather to instill fear. This amounted to torture, according to Teresa Kok, a member of the Malaysian parliament. After Gadaffi died, Kok expressed her condolences to his family and asked, "How come other teachers and adults did not intervene when the students were tortured?"[57]

> "I'm not normal anymore."[58]
>
> —Younous Chekkouri, a former Guantánamo Bay detainee

Psychological Damage

Torture leaves emotional scars as well. Follow-up studies of torture victims have found that many suffer from long-lasting psychological damage, including anxiety disorders, depression, irritability, shame, memory impairment, amnesia, a reduced capacity

"I Can't Forget"

According to the Syrian Network for Human Rights, the Syrian government has tortured thousands of Syrians since civil war broke out in 2011. One torture victim, identified only as Yehia, told his story to Al Jazeera, a media network:

> I was blindfolded and my hands and feet were tied. Sometimes they would use electric cables and give us electric shocks. They would beat us with iron rods after pouring water on our bodies so that it hurts more. . . . One officer jammed a rod in my knee so hard that it's left a permanent injury in my leg.
>
> I was scared of dying. I was scared.
>
> The voice of the women from the next cell haunted me more. There were at least 50 women next door. The screams of those women were unbearable. . . . I can't forget it.
>
> One day, while I was being moved from one prison to another, I peered through from under my blindfold. I saw a young man, probably 24–25 years old, lying on the floor with his head next to the drain. Something was leaking from it and I realised it was blood. . . . I can't shut that image out of my head.

Quoted in Priyanka Gupta, "'It Was Hell': Syrian Refugees Share Stories of Torture," Al Jazeera, June 25, 2016. www .aljazeera.com.

to concentrate, headaches, sleep disturbances and nightmares, emotional instability, sexual problems, self-mutilation, a preoccupation with suicide, and social isolation. Younous Chekkouri is one such victim who continues to suffer the lingering effects of his abuse. Chekkouri was a Moroccan who was living in Afghanistan at the time of the 9/11 terrorist attacks. A suspected al Qaeda fighter, he was captured by Pakistani forces as he fled Afghanistan in December 2001. The Pakistanis turned Chekkouri over to US forces, which placed him in a US military jail in Kandahar. Chekkouri says he was beaten several times and was forced to watch his younger brother be beaten as well. He was transferred to Guantánamo Bay in 2002, where he remained until his release in 2015. He says he has flashbacks to his time in prison, seeing faces of his Guantánamo guards in crowds when he leaves his home. "I am living this kind of depression," says Chekkouri. "I'm not normal anymore."[58]

> "I have been suffering from absent-mindedness, amnesia, inability to memorize, depression, helplessness, apathy, loss of interest in the future, slow thinking, and anxiety."[60]
>
> —Khaled El-Masri, a former CIA detainee

For years it was believed there were no long-term consequences from enhanced interrogation techniques or the use of so-called white torture. In fact, lawyers at the US Justice Department who approved the use of enhanced interrogation techniques did so in part because they found no evidence that such methods would have a lasting impact on detainees. In 2016, however, the *New York Times* reported that detainees who were subjected to enhanced interrogation in secret CIA prisons and at Guantánamo Bay have since shown long-term psychiatric problems and mental health issues. "Some emerged with the same symptoms as American prisoners of war who were brutalized decades earlier by some of the world's cruelest regimes," write reporters Matt Apuzzo, Sheri Fink, and James Risen. They continue:

> Today in Slovakia, Hussein al-Marfadi describes permanent headaches and disturbed sleep, plagued by memories of dogs inside a blackened jail. In Kazakhstan, Lutfi bin Ali is haunted by nightmares of suffocating at the bottom of a well. In Libya, the radio from a passing car spurs rage in Majid Mokhtar Sasy al-Maghrebi, reminding him of the C.I.A. prison where earsplitting music was just one assault to his senses.[59]

Khaled El-Masri is a former CIA detainee who reports long-term psychological damage. In a case of mistaken identity, El-Masri, a German citizen, was arrested by Macedonian authorities in 2003 and was turned over to American authorities. El-Masri says his captors stripped him naked, forced a suppository into his anus, and beat him repeatedly. Released in 2004, El-Masri told the *New York Times* that he continues to have nightmares that are accompanied by a feeling of tightness in his chest. He added, "I have been suffering from absent-mindedness, amnesia, inability to memorize, depression, helplessness, apathy, loss of interest in the future, slow thinking, and anxiety."[60]

Those in a victim's life often suffer too. The spouses of torture victims are more prone to depression. The children of torture victims sometimes are affected as well. Ben Soud, a Libyan who had joined an Islamist movement aimed at overthrowing Libya's late dictator, Muammar el-Qaddafi, was arrested in Pakistan in 2003 and was turned over to the CIA as a suspected terrorist. Soud says the interrogators mistreated him in several ways, including shackling him in stress positions, shoving him into a wall, and locking him in a coffin-sized box. Released from captivity in 2011, Soud says he is filled with self-doubt, finds it hard to make decisions, and experiences mood swings. He told the *New*

Khaled el-Masri, a former CIA detainee, says he was beaten, stripped naked, and subjected to other treatment that has left him with long-term psychological problems including nightmares, depression, and anxiety.

York Times that his children sometimes ask, "'Dad, why did you suddenly get angry?' 'Why did you suddenly snap?'" Answering those questions, he says, would involve revealing what he went through. "How can you explain such things to children?"[61] he asks.

Long-Lasting Consequences

Torture does not have to last for a long time to make a deep impression on the victim. In 2016 the Istanbul Protocol Project in the Basque Country Working Group interviewed forty-five torture victims from the Basque area of northern Spain and southwestern France who had been detained by the Spanish authorities. The authorities suspected them of being members or supporters of the armed Basque separatist group Euskadi Ta Askatasuna, and they were imprisoned without the ability to speak with family

A Torturer Describes His Guilt

Iraq War veteran Daniel Keller spoke with American RadioWorks about the guilt he feels about how he treated detainees:

> Every once in a while I get to these points where I can't sleep. . . . And that's when you really start thinking about it is when you're there, alone, at night, in bed, staring at the ceiling and you're thinking about all the bad stuff you did. . . .

> There's a lot of stuff that you're not even supposed to do that you do over there. And you know, of course it raises the morality issues. Did you know that you couldn't do it? Does it matter? Is it something that you should have known that you couldn't do? It makes you wonder, you know, did I do this because of the stress? Did I do this because of the situation? Should I have known not to do this anyway? Am I at fault here? You know, and if I am, does that make me a bad person? A lot of your emotional ramifications come from these feelings of guilt. . . .

> What was terrible [about seeing the photographs in the news from the Abu Ghraib prison] was seeing what I was doing outside of myself. It was like having an opportunity to be there watching myself do it, you know? And that is pretty God awful to actually have to come to terms visually with what you're doing.

Quoted in American RadioWorks, "What Killed Sergeant Gray," American Public Media, 2010. http://americanradio works.publicradio.org.

members, lawyers, or their own doctors. Their confinement was relatively brief. More than half of the detainees (53.3 percent) were held for just five days. The longest detention lasted ten days. But in that time, all participants in the study were tortured. Some were beaten; some were shocked with electricity; some were forced to undress and were sexually assaulted. Almost all of the participants were subjected to *la bolsa* ("the bag"), a torture technique in which a plastic bag is placed over the face and head for a period of time, making it difficult or impossible for the victim to breathe.

As a result of this treatment, researchers found that 53 percent of the torture victims exhibited symptoms of post-traumatic stress disorder (PTSD); 13.4 percent were diagnosed with depressive disorder; 6.7 percent had an anxiety disorder; and 6.7 percent suffered from somatoform disorder, a mental disorder in which a patient experiences physical symptoms that cannot be fully explained by any underlying general medical condition.

The Basque torture victims presented an array of PTSD symptoms. Some suffered from a condition known as reexperiencing, or feeling as if the event was happening again. "When a stimulus reminds me what happened (a smell, looks, body shape), it makes me jump, my heart races, I experience again all the emotions provoked in torture," says one detainee. "Even today I feel fear when those feelings and emotions come to my head; it still makes a knot in my stomach, I still cry just by the mere memory of what I have lived through and felt."[62]

Many of the Basque victims feel distant from other people. "Relations with people were wrong, rare, and very different from what they were before,"[63] explains one torture victim. "I get sick when we are with a lot of people," says another. "They were telling me things and I felt like . . . it's that I have nothing to say. What do I say?"[64] Other victims describe a deep, irrational distrust of others. "Lot of times I think that I'm going to be arrested or I get nervous. I just look at someone and think 'How strange he looks.' I get very nervous: 'Why is that guy looking at me?'"[65] Sometimes the distrust turns to anger, as this victim reports: "I become very suspicious and I feel very aggressive. . . . I get angry too easily, I get mad. If someone grabs me from behind to hug me I can react very badly and I can even react giving him a punch."[66] Loss of temper is common. Another victim says, "I was much quieter, now I get out of control when something happens or offends me."[67]

The Effects on Torturers

Victims are not the only ones who suffer long-term mental and emotional damage from torture. Torturers suffer as well. "I tortured people," Tony Lagouranis, an American military intelligence specialist who served in Iraq from January 2004 until January 2005, told the *Washington Post*. "You have to twist your mind up so much to justify doing that." Lagouranis emerged from his experience confused and fearful. "You don't know if you'll ever regain a sense of self," he said. "I used to have a strong sense of morals. I was on the side of good. I don't even understand the sides anymore."[68]

Adam Stevenson, who also served as an interrogator in Iraq, suffered from PTSD symptoms, including nightmares and a loss of interest in work. When his tour of duty ended in 2004, Stevenson went to school to study law enforcement. He was offered a job with the sheriff's department in Riverside, California, but he declined the opportunity when he learned that the position would involve working in the jail. "Never mind," he told his prospective employer. "I hate working with detainees."[69] Stevenson found that he simply could not do work that reminded him of his experiences in Iraq.

> "I tortured people. You have to twist your mind up so much to justify doing that."[68]
>
> —Tony Lagouranis, an American military intelligence specialist

"Toxic Levels of Guilt and Shame"

In his book *None of Us Were Like This Before: American Soldiers and Torture*, Joshua E.S. Phillips tells compelling stories of American soldiers who abused Iraqi detainees. Many now suffer from addiction, depression, self-loathing, and what Darius Rejali, a professor at Reed College, in Portland, Oregon, calls "toxic levels of guilt and shame."[70]

One such person was Adam James Gray, a sergeant in the US Army who served in a tank battalion in Iraq. His unit eventually became responsible for detaining prisoners. Trained for combat, not prisoner supervision, members of Gray's unit routinely abused Iraqis suspected of being insurgents. Oral Lindsey, Gray's tank commander, explains how many soldiers lost their moral compass when confronted with the task of dealing with prisoners who

US soldiers carry comrades who were killed by a roadside-bomb blast in Afghanistan. Soldiers sometimes lose their moral compass when dealing with prisoners who built the bombs that killed their friends and colleagues.

were suspected of building explosives and engaging in other warfare. "You lose your morals, man," says Lindsey. "I mean . . . he's out there making bombs, you know? He's out there trying to kill you and all you want to do is go home to your family, so hey. You do what you gotta do, you know?"[71]

According to Daniel Keller, who served alongside Gray and Lindsey, combat fundamentally changed him and the other members of his unit. "None of us were like this before," he says. "No one thought about, you know, dragging people through concertina [barbed] wire or beating them or sandbagging them or strangling them or you know, anything like that . . . before this."[72] Professor Rejali agrees. "Basically they're normal when they go in. They're not sadists," he says of the soldiers. "They're chosen primarily because they're loyal, they're patriotic, and they can keep a secret."[73]

Gray was particularly haunted by things he did to detainees in Iraq, included depriving them of sleep with bright lights and loud music, suspending them by their wrists, and frightening them by blindfolding them, taking them into rooms with walls covered with chicken blood, and then removing the blindfolds. Army psychiatrists observed that Gray "experienced poor sleep, decreased appetite, stomachaches, headaches, and hypervigilance" after returning from Iraq. Army doctors concluded that Gray suffered from PTSD, and his psychiatric report noted the following:

> Gray was upset by thoughts of not being a good NCO [noncommissioned officer]. Gray said that those problems were due to the way he felt about what happened to him during his deployment. Gray said that he could not sleep without alcohol, and that the last time he did sleep without alcohol, he woke up screaming with the sheets soaked with his sweat.[74]

A few months after Gray returned from Iraq, he was found dead in his barracks with a plastic bag over his head. The army ruled his death an accident, but those who knew him suspected suicide. Jonathan Millantz, a combat medic who served with Gray, believes Gray's feelings about his actions in Iraq contributed to his death. "It haunts me every day, and it's something I'll never get away from—and it's been four years since I was over there," says Millantz. "It's something that I'm sure it took a toll on Adam [Gray]."[75]

Chapter 5

What Can Be Done to Reduce Torture?

Focus Questions

1. To what extent does journalism that exposes torture actually help to reduce it?

2. Should high-ranking officials be prosecuted for ordering torture even if they believed it was lawful? Explain your answer.

3. Should governments pay reparations to known terrorists if they were tortured while being detained? Why or why not?

Despite more than a dozen international agreements prohibiting torture and almost universal official condemnation of the practice, Amnesty International reports that at least 122 countries and some independent organizations currently use torture to intimidate, silence, punish, or interrogate. This suggests that treaties prohibiting torture need to be better enforced and that other tools need be adopted to reduce the use of torture worldwide.

Exposing Torture Where It Occurs

Because torture is broadly condemned, it is usually practiced in secret. As a result, many efforts to prevent torture center on exposing it to the world community. Members of human rights organizations such as Amnesty International and Human Rights Watch scour the world to learn about abuses. When they find them, the organizations issue press releases and annual reports describing the incidents.

Journalists also inform the public about torture and cruel, inhuman, and degrading treatment. For example, in October 2016 the Australian Broadcasting Corporation (ABC) broadcast a televised exposé entitled "The Forgotten Children: Four Corners Visits Nauru," detailing abuses of people fleeing oppression in countries such as Syria and Myanmar and trying to make their way to Australia. Many of these people, known as refugees, were turned away and sent to the island nation of Nauru. Under international law, the refugees could not be returned to their home countries because they might be harmed there. The government of Nauru placed the more than 700 refugees—including more than 120 children and teenagers—in detention camps. Anya Niestat, the senior director of research for Amnesty International, reported that conditions in the camps were horrible.

Evan Davies, a schoolteacher on the island, told ABC that the purpose of the camp was not simply to hold the detainees and their children but also to punish them. "The whole way that the camp was set up was simply to break the kids' spirits, and the asylum seekers' spirits. There is no question about that. It was torture."[76] Amnesty International agreed with Davies's assessment, stating, "The conditions on Nauru—refugees' severe mental anguish, the intentional nature of the system, and the fact that the goal of offshore processing is to intimidate or coerce people to achieve a specific outcome amounts to torture."[77]

Making Torture Seem Normal

Some human rights experts question the value of telling these stories. They worry that exposing the many instances of torture can actually make torture seem normal. The more normal a behavior appears, the more it is typically accepted, and the less it is condemned. As a result, some argue that simply exposing examples of torture does not actually serve to reduce it. "While human rights groups such as Amnesty International and Human Rights Watch work hard to discover and publicize human rights abuses, I am not aware of any research, either by human rights nonprofits or by scholars, that shows that these strategies actually work [to reduce torture],"[78] writes Christopher J. Einolf, a professor at DePaul University in Chicago who specializes in torture research.

News reports and international criticism may cause a regime to change the type of torture it uses, but they do not appear to end torture's use. In fact, this may only encourage entities that torture to find ways to cover up their actions. "Existing research

Hundreds of Syrians flee violence-torn regions of their country. Journalists are often the ones who tell the heart-wrenching stories of fleeing refugees.

has found that international criticism leads regimes to switch from torture methods that leave scars to torture methods that are less easy to detect,"[79] writes Einholf. James Ron, a professor of international affairs at the University of Minnesota, found that intense scrutiny from the media and human rights organizations caused Israel's security forces to change their interrogation methods.

> In the early years a majority of interrogation subjects were subjected to severe beatings, many of which involved broken bones and hospitalization. Under the new system, however, bones rarely were broken and the intensity of direct physical force had dropped. Interrogators introduced and refined a complex package of methods including beatings that left no marks, painful body positioning, and sensory deprivation.[80]

Amnesty International's 12-Point Program for the Prevention of Torture

The human rights organization Amnesty International has developed a 12-point program that can help governments prevent torture:

1. Have high-level government officials condemn the use of torture in all situations.
2. Make sure that relatives, lawyers, and doctors can visit prisoners.
3. Eliminate secret prisons.
4. Provide prisoners with legal safeguards, such as being informed of their rights.
5. Pass laws that make torture a crime in that country.
6. Investigate all reports of torture to see if they are true.
7. Prosecute those who conducted or ordered torture.
8. Ban the use of any statement made by a person being tortured (if victims' statements cannot be used, then there is less reason to torture people).
9. Provide training for the people who are involved in arresting and questioning prisoners about what constitutes torture and cruel, inhuman, and degrading treatment.
10. Create a system to provide reparations to torture victims.
11. Agree to and ratify international treaties banning torture and other ill treatment.
12. Encourage governments to get involved when torture is reported in other countries.

Sometimes news about torture causes public outrage, leading some people to demonstrate against the practice. Researchers have found that when such dissent turns violent and threatens to overthrow the government, it does not serve to eliminate torture. Instead, the government officials tend to resist changing their methods even more. "States rarely terminate the use of torture when they face a threat,"[81] write political scientists Courtenay Ryals Conrad and Will H. Moore.

What does seem to decrease the use of torture is when a country moves from an authoritarian form of government to a more open, democratic form. According to Conrad and Moore, "States with popular suffrage and a free press are considerably more likely to terminate their use of torture." In a study of sixty-four countries, Conrad and Moore found that countries that experienced greater freedom of the press were much more likely to decrease torture than countries where freedom of the press did not change. They write,

> A country moving from restricted to partly free, or partly free to free is nearly 95% more likely to terminate its use of torture; one that moves from restricted to free is 190% more likely to terminate its use of torture (relative to continuing to torture). . . . Mali and Thailand terminated the use of torture in the year in which they transitioned from autocracy to democracy. The termination of torture in Greece coincided with a change in executive leadership.[82]

Reducing the Conditions That Facilitate Torture

While the movement toward a more open society can reduce the use of torture, such changes can take many years. Rather than wait for such sweeping social changes to take effect, human rights groups have identified steps that governments should take to eliminate the conditions that make torture more likely. For example, Amnesty International's 12-Point Program for the Prevention of Torture calls for an end to secret detention, such as CIA black sites and the incommunicado detention practiced in Spain. Simply allowing friends, family, and doctors to visit prisoners and detainees makes torture less likely. "Torture and other ill-treatment often take place while prisoners are held incommunicado— unable to contact people outside who could help them or find out what is happening to them," states Amnesty International. "The practice of incommunicado detention should be ended."[83]

"States with popular suffrage and a free press are considerably more likely to terminate their use of torture."[82]

—Courtenay Ryals Conrad and Will H. Moore, political scientists

Another condition that can reduce torture, according to Amnesty International, is instituting legal safeguards during detention and interrogation. In other words, governments should be required to tell detainees why they are being held, what charges they face, and when they will have a hearing. "All prisoners should be immediately informed of their rights," states Amnesty International. "These include the right to lodge complaints about their treatment and to have a judge rule without delay on the lawfulness of their detention."[84]

Improve Monitoring

Many of the countries that torture people are not open societies and are not likely to become more open or adopt antitorture reforms on their own. However, many of those countries have signed international agreements, such as the UN Convention Against Torture. As a result, the UN monitors actions in those countries to make sure torture is not occurring. One of the offices involved with such oversight is the Office of the United Nations High Commissioner for Human Rights (OHCHR).

The OHCHR states that there are three steps to eliminating torture: establishing a legal framework to prohibit it, effectively implementing that framework, and setting up mechanisms to monitor the framework and its implementation. The first step includes getting countries to ratify antitorture agreements, such as the UN Convention Against Torture. The second step involves creating agencies that have the authority to enforce laws against torture. The third step is for international agencies to ensure that prohibitions are being enforced.

The third step is the most difficult, in part because the UN lacks the legal authority to monitor torture. "UN human rights committees hold an ambiguous position in international law. Although they are at the center of the international human rights system, they lack the ability to determine issues of fact, or to issue legally binding decisions," writes Tobias Kelly, a professor of social anthropology at the University of Edinburgh in Scotland. "Furthermore, although the Committee members are supposed to monitor compliance, they do not have the resources to launch effective investigations."[85] Instead, UN committees rely on nongovernmental organizations, such as Amnesty International and Human Rights Watch, to gather information. The UN committees then present this information to the various governments accused of human rights abuses.

For example, when the UN Committee Against Torture met with American officials in 2006, it recommended that the United

Israeli security forces arrest Palestinians during clashes in the West Bank in 2017. Intense public scrutiny led Israel to change its interrogation methods.

States "rescind any interrogation technique, including methods involving sexual humiliation, 'waterboarding,' [and] 'short shack-ling.'"[86] In 2009 the United States did so. Similarly, acting on information from Amnesty International and local groups in the African nation of Togo, the Committee Against Torture met with government officials and discussed the "numerous reports containing allegations of acts of torture and cruel, inhuman, and degrading treatment submitted to the Committee."[87] In 2016 Togo's national assembly passed a law that defined torture in line with the UN Convention Against Torture and made it a crime.

Punish the Torturers

Many experts believe that a crucial element in reducing torture is to bring torturers to justice, either through their own country's legal system or before an international court. In the event a nation fails to prosecute its officials for violating torture laws, the person accused of torture might face criminal charges abroad before the International Criminal Court or even before the court of a foreign power.

Reparations Gone Wrong

In 2010 the British government paid more than $25 million to former detainees to compensate them for their suffering at the Guantánamo Bay prison. However, some in the United Kingdom have criticized that decision. They believe it was a mistake to give large amounts of money to suspected terrorists, citing the case of a former Guantánamo Bay detainee named Jamal al-Harith.

Born Ronald Fiddler in Manchester, England, al-Harith was picked up as a suspected terrorist by American forces in Kabul, Afghanistan. The US Army sent al-Harith to the Guantánamo Bay detention center, where he said he was subjected to cruel and degrading treatment. In 2004 he was released from the prison, returned to the United Kingdom, and became one of sixteen former detainees who were awarded reparations by the British government.

Four years later al-Harith used that money to travel to Syria, where he joined the Islamic State's paramilitary forces. In February 2017 a video surfaced showing al-Harith driving a car packed full of explosives toward an Iraqi army base southwest of Mosul on a suicide bombing mission. The Islamic State released a statement claiming that al-Harith had succeeded in carrying out the attack. Western sources could not confirm the statement, but the Associated Press reported that a series of suicide bombings in that area of Mosul on that day killed at least seven soldiers. Tim Houghton, a member of the British parliament, called al-Harith's payment a "scandalous situation." A former neighbor of the suicide bomber was even blunter: "We have paid him to become a terrorist."

Quoted in Kathryn Blackhurst, "Detainee Released from Gitmo Turns ISIS Suicide Bomber," LifeZette, February 22, 2017. www.lifezette.com.

For example, in 1999 a Spanish court charged General Augusto Pinochet, the ruler of Chile between 1973 and 1990, with thirty-four counts of torture. The Spanish court said it was able to prosecute Pinochet for these crimes because of a principle known as universal jurisdiction, which allows countries or international organizations to claim criminal jurisdiction over an accused person regardless of where the alleged crime was committed, the person's nationality, or where he or she lives. Even though Pinochet died before the Spanish court could convict him of any crimes, universal jurisdiction offers a way for countries to prosecute people suspected of torture even if they live outside of their geographical boundaries.

Although universal jurisdiction succeeded in the Pinochet case, it has limitations as a tool with which to punish torturers. The main problem is getting torturers to appear before a court in a foreign country. In the Pinochet case, the British courts ruled that Pinochet should be extradited, or handed over to Spanish authorities to face trial. In Britain, the United States, and many other countries, a person being sought for extradition has the right to a hearing before a judge, with all the safeguards of the legal system. The evidence of wrongdoing must be substantial and in accordance with the laws of the country where the defendant is living. In the case of torture, it would have to be shown that the accused person committed torture according to his or her own country's laws.

For example, many human rights advocates have called for former president George W. Bush and members of his administration to be brought before international courts on charges of authorizing torture. "Torture is a crime and those responsible for crimes must be brought to justice," says Steven W. Hawkins, executive director of Amnesty International USA. "Former President George W. Bush should have been investigated long ago for his role in authorizing this program, including his assertion since leaving office that he personally granted the CIA's request to use waterboarding and other 'enhanced interrogation techniques' against particular detainees."[88]

However, at an extradition hearing, the Department of Justice memo stating that enhanced interrogation techniques are legal would be strong evidence that neither Bush nor his subordinates authorized torture or broke any American laws. In addition, a 2006 federal law known as the Military Commissions Act shields some US officials from allegations of torture. As David Cole of the American Civil Liberties Union puts it, "Criminal prosecution within or outside the United States is highly unlikely. At home, the Justice Department's 'torture memo' would be a legal defense for any but the lawyers who wrote it, and Congress, in the Military Commissions Act, granted retrospective immunity to officials involved in the interrogation of al-Qaeda suspects in the wake of September 11."[89]

> "Torture is a crime and those responsible for crimes must be brought to justice."[88]
>
> —Steven W. Hawkins, executive director of Amnesty International USA

Reparations

While extradition law makes it difficult to bring officials to justice for practicing or authorizing torture, governments themselves can be punished for such acts. For example, they can be required to pay compensation to the victims, known as reparations. Several torture victims have successfully sued governments for reparations. For example, sixteen former Guantánamo Bay detainees sued the British government for reparations in 2010. Rather than have the case go to trial, where national security details might be revealed to the public, the British government agreed to pay the detainees £20 million ($25.9 million) in reparations.

In 2012 the European Court of Human Rights ordered the government of Macedonia to pay Khaled El-Masri $80,000 as compensation for his mistreatment at the hands of Macedonian authorities, who turned him over to the CIA. The court ruled that El-Masri's

Lawsuits are one way to bring the topic of torture out into the open. Lawyers for detainees who have been tortured say that those who engage in torture must be held accountable for their actions.

rights were violated when he was shackled, hooded, subjected to sensory deprivation, and forcibly removed from an area by Macedonian security agents. El-Masri's attorney, Darian Pavli, said the ruling was a "signal to all countries who are planning to collaborate with the US that these practices cannot be justified and that their governments and individuals will be held responsible."[90]

Other lawsuits are proceeding. In 2016 a high court in Denmark ruled that eleven Iraqis could sue the Danish Ministry of Defence for damages related to their alleged torture during a military operation run by Danish soldiers in Basra, Iraq, in 2004.

Similar lawsuits have been brought directly against the United States, with mixed results. Several courts have dismissed such lawsuits because the Military Commissions Act created special military courts to hear the cases of enemy combatants. For this reason, a three-judge panel of the US Court of Appeals barred a former detainee named Mohammed Jawad from suing for damages in US courts. However, in January 2017 a US District Court judge in Seattle, Justin L. Quackenbush, allowed a similar lawsuit to move forward. The suit involves former detainees who were held in overseas prisons by the CIA. They are not suing the US government but instead are suing two American psychologists who helped devise the CIA's enhanced interrogation program. The detainees claim the techniques used were torture. Quackenbush ruled that the psychologists failed to show that the three men were properly detained as enemy combatants, which would have meant they were covered by the Military Commissions Act. Quackenbush also ruled that the psychologists failed to show that they acted as agents of the US government, which would have shielded them from such a lawsuit. "This ruling sends the strong signal that anyone who participates in shameful and unlawful government torture can't count on escaping accountability in a court of law," said Dror Ladin, an attorney for the former detainees. "The court's decision . . . confirms that our clients can continue their fight to hold accountable the psychologists who devised and profited from the C.I.A. torture program."[91]

"Anyone who participates in shameful and unlawful government torture can't count on escaping accountability in a court of law."[91]

—Dror Ladin, a staff attorney with the American Civil Liberties Union

Human rights experts have offered many ideas for how to reduce torture, and some progress has been made. Five hundred years ago, torture was considered a normal part of society. Less than one hundred years ago, there were no international laws against torture. Today it is considered a crime against humanity. Nevertheless, much work remains to be done. Perhaps the most important thing is for each person to take some responsibility for ending it. As author, professor, and Nobel Peace laureate Elie Wiesel once wrote,

We must take sides. Neutrality helps the oppressor, never the victim. Silence encourages the tormentor, never the tormented. Sometimes we must interfere. When human lives are endangered, when human dignity is in jeopardy, national borders and sensitivities become irrelevant. Wherever men and women are persecuted because of their race, religion, or political views, that place must—at that moment—become the center of the universe.[92]

Source Notes

Introduction: A Darkening World

1. United Nations, "Declaration of Human Rights." www.un.org.
2. Human Rights Watch, "The Legal Prohibition Against Torture," March 11, 2003. www.hrw.org.
3. Quoted in Joshua Cole, "Intimate Acts and Unspeakable Relations: Remembering Torture and the War for Algerian Independence," in *Memory, Empire, and Postcolonialism: Legacies of French Colonialism,* ed. Alec G. Hargreaves. Lanham, MD: Lexington, 2005, p. 132.
4. Quoted in Australian Broadcasting Corporation, "Britain Admits 1950s Torture of Kenyans," July 18, 2012. www.abc.net.au.
5. Quoted in Australian Broadcasting Corporation, "Britain Admits 1950s Torture of Kenyans."
6. Quoted in Sam Creighton and David Connett, "Cyprus Fighters Sue Britain for Torture During Uprising," *Independent* (London), December 2, 2012. www.independent.co.uk.
7. Quoted in Amnesty International, "Global Crisis on Torture Exposed by New Worldwide Campaign," May 13, 2014. www.amnesty.org.

Chapter 1: Torture in the Twenty-First Century

8. Christian Meyer et al., "The Massacre Mass Grave of Schöneck-Kilianstädten Reveals New Insights into Collective Violence in Early Neolithic Central Europe," *Proceedings of the National Academy of Sciences of the United States of America*, September 8, 2015. www.ncbi.nlm.nih.gov.
9. Quoted in John Davidson, "Beaten and Bruised, Detainee Recounts Islamic State Torture," Reuters, December 1, 2016. www.reuters.com.
10. Amnesty International, *"Welcome to Hell Fire": Torture and Other Ill-Treatment in Nigeria*. London: Amnesty International, 2014, p. 6.

11. Quoted in Amnesty International, *"Welcome to Hell Fire,"* p. 13.
12. Ruth Seifert, *War and Rape. Analytical Approaches*. Geneva, Switzerland: Women's International League for Peace and Freedom, p. 1.
13. Quoted in Human Rights Watch, "Iraq: Sunni Women Tell of ISIS Detention, Torture," February 20, 2017. www.hrw.org.
14. Quoted in Andrew Osborn, "Mass Rape Ruled a War Crime," *Guardian* (Manchester), February 23, 2001. www.theguardian.com.
15. Sam Johnson and Jan Winebrenner, *Captive Warriors: A Vietnam POW's Story*. College Station: Texas A&M University Press, 1992, p. 84.
16. John S. McCain, "John McCain, Prisoner of War: A First-Person Account," *U.S. News & World Report*, January 28, 2008. www.usnews.com.
17. Steven W. Hawkins, "Release of Torture Report Underscores Need for Accountability," Amnesty International, press release, December 9, 2014. www.amnestyusa.org.
18. Quoted in Jim Snyder, "Terror Suspects Doused with Water, Force-Fed Rectally by CIA," Bloomberg, December 10, 2014. www.bloomberg.com.
19. Quoted in Office of the Press Secretary, "Press Conference by the President," White House, August 1, 2014. https://obamawhitehouse.archives.gov.
20. Quoted in Peter Baker, "Dismissing Senate Report, Cheney Defends C.I.A. Interrogations," *New York Times*, December 8, 2014. www.nytimes.com.
21. Quoted in Baker, "Dismissing Senate Report, Cheney Defends C.I.A. Interrogations."
22. Quoted in Amnesty International, "40th Anniversary Peter Benenson Quote," September 30, 2001. www.amnesty.org.
23. Quoted in Saleh Hamid, "Kurdish Prisoner to Khamenei: 'I Was Raped by Your Interrogators,'" Al-Arabiya.net, March 28, 2017. http://english.alarabiya.net.
24. Quoted in Peter Zhi, "'A Human Rights Scourge': Canada's Role in the Struggle Against Torture," *McGill Daily* (Montréal), February 3, 2015. www.mcgilldaily.com.

Chapter 2: What Constitutes Torture?

25. *Amnesty International Report 2016/17*, p. 52. www.amnesty.org.

26. United Nations, "Convention Against Torture and Other Inhuman or Degrading Treatment or Punishment." www.ohchr.org.

27. Quoted in Shawn Walker, "Chechens Tell of Prison Beatings and Electric Shocks in Anti-Gay Purge: 'They Called Us Animals,'" *Guardian* (Manchester), April 13, 2017. www.theguardian.com.

28. Quoted in Walker, "Chechens Tell of Prison Beatings and Electric Shocks in Anti-Gay Purge."

29. Quoted in Mark Lowen, "Turkey Torture Claims in Wake of Failed Coup," BBC News, November 28, 2016. www.bbc.com.

30. Quoted in Human Rights Watch, "Torture Archipelago," July 3, 2012. www.hrw.org.

31. Mohamedou Ould Slahi, "The Guantánamo Memoirs of Mohamedou Ould Slahi," *Slate*, May 2, 2013. www.slate.com.

32. Cole, "Intimate Acts and Unspeakable Relations," p. 133.

33. Quoted in Istanbul Protocol Project in the Basque Country Working Group, *Incommunicado Detention and Torture in Spain*, 2016, p. 100. http://tbinternet.ohchr.org.

34. Quoted in Lowen, "Turkey Torture Claims in Wake of Failed Coup."

35. Quoted in Steven Nelson, "Detainee Fed Through Rectum Was Raped, His Attorney Says," *U.S. News & World Report*, December 10, 2014. www.usnews.com.

36. Quoted in Lowen, "Turkey Torture Claims in Wake of Failed Coup."

37. Quoted in Istanbul Protocol Project in the Basque Country Working Group, *Incommunicado Detention and Torture in Spain*, p. 97.

38. Quoted in American RadioWorks, "What Killed Sergeant Gray," American Public Media, 2010. http://americanradioworks.publicradio.org.

39. Slahi, "The Guantánamo Memoirs of Mohamedou Ould Slahi."

40. Human Rights Watch, "The Legal Prohibition Against Torture."

41. Human Rights Watch, "The Legal Prohibition Against Torture."

Chapter 3: Is Torture Ever Justified?

42. Quoted in Matt Ford, "Antonin Scalia's Case for Torture," *Atlantic*, December 13, 2014. www.theatlantic.com.
43. Quoted in Ford, "Antonin Scalia's Case for Torture."
44. Gary Gutting and Jeff McMahan, "Can Torture Ever Be Moral?," *Opinionator* (blog), *New York Times*, January 26, 2015. http://opinionator.blogs.nytimes.com.
45. Quoted in Barry Gewen, "Thinking the Unthinkable," *New York Times*, September 15, 2002. www.nytimes.com.
46. United Nations, "Convention Against Torture and Other Inhuman or Degrading Treatment or Punishment."
47. Quoted in International Committee of the Red Cross, "Treaties, States Parties and Commentaries." https://ihl-databases.icrc.org.
48. Quoted in International Committee of the Red Cross, "Treaties, States Parties and Commentaries."
49. Quoted in Brad Knickerbocker, "Can Torture Be Justified?," *Christian Science Monitor*, May 19, 2004. www.csmonitor.com.
50. Quoted in Knickerbocker, "Can Torture Be Justified?"
51. Quoted in Knickerbocker, "Can Torture Be Justified?"
52. George W. Bush, *Decision Points*. New York: Crown, 2010, p. 180.
53. Abu Abdillah Almoravid, "Shattered: A Story About Change," *Inspire*, Spring 2014, p. 53. https://azelin.files.wordpress.com.
54. Quoted in Laura Blumenfeld, "The Tortured Lives of Interrogators," *Washington Post*, June 4, 2007. www.washingtonpost.com.

Chapter 4: The Consequences of Torture

55. Quoted in Joshua E.S. Phillips, *None of Us Were Like This Before: American Soldiers and Torture*. London: Verso, 2012, p. 27.
56. Quoted in Halim Said, "Boy's Legs Amputated After Alleged Whipping by Religious School Warden," *New Straits Times* (Kuala Lampur, Malaysia), April 22, 2017. https://sg.news.yahoo.com.
57. Quoted in Danial Albakri and Ashley Tang, "Condolences Pour In over Mohamad Thaqif's Death," *Toronto Star*, April 26, 2017. www.thestar.com.
58. Quoted in Matt Apuzzo, Sheri Fink, and James Risen, "How U.S. Torture Left a Legacy of Damaged Minds," *New York Times*, October 9, 2016. www.nytimes.com.

59. Apuzzo, Fink, and Risen, "How U.S. Torture Left a Legacy of Damaged Minds."
60. Quoted in Apuzzo, Fink, and Risen, "How U.S. Torture Left a Legacy of Damaged Minds."
61. Quoted in Apuzzo, Fink, and Risen, "How U.S. Torture Left a Legacy of Damaged Minds."
62. Quoted in Istanbul Protocol Project in the Basque Country Working Group, *Incommunicado Detention and Torture in Spain*, p. 171.
63. Quoted in Istanbul Protocol Project in the Basque Country Working Group, *Incommunicado Detention and Torture in Spain*, p. 175.
64. Quoted in Istanbul Protocol Project in the Basque Country Working Group, *Incommunicado Detention and Torture in Spain*, p. 175.
65. Quoted in Istanbul Protocol Project in the Basque Country Working Group, *Incommunicado Detention and Torture in Spain*, p. 177.
66. Quoted in Istanbul Protocol Project in the Basque Country Working Group, *Incommunicado Detention and Torture in Spain*, p. 178.
67. Quoted in Istanbul Protocol Project in the Basque Country Working Group, *Incommunicado Detention and Torture in Spain*, p. 178.
68. Quoted in Blumenfeld, "The Tortured Lives of Interrogators."
69. Quoted in Phillips, *None of Us Were Like This Before*, p. 131.
70. Quoted in Lydia DePillis, "This Is How It Feels to Torture," *Washington Post*, December 11, 2014. www.washington post.com.
71. Quoted in American RadioWorks, "What Killed Sergeant Gray."
72. Quoted in American RadioWorks, "What Killed Sergeant Gray."
73. Quoted in DePillis, "This Is How It Feels to Torture."
74. Quoted in Phillips, *None of Us Were Like This Before*, p. 15.
75. Quoted in American RadioWorks, "What Killed Sergeant Gray."

Chapter 5: What Can Be Done to Reduce Torture?

76. Quoted in Australian Broadcasting Corporation News, "The Forgotten Children: Four Corners Visits Nauru," YouTube, October 17, 2016. https://youtu.be/com/4uakOJL2Esw.
77. Amnesty International, *Island of Despair*. London: Amnesty International, 2016, p. 7.

78. Christopher J. Einolf, "Preventing Torture," *Torture Research*, January 27, 2010. https://tortureresearch.wordpress.com.
79. Einolf, "Preventing Torture."
80. James Ron, "Varying Methods of State Violence," *International Organization*, Spring 1997, p. 275–76. http://jamesron.com.
81. Courtenay Ryals Conrad and Will H. Moore, "What Stops the Torture?," *American Journal of Political Science*, April 9, 2010, p. 459.
82. Conrad and Moore, "What Stops the Torture?," pp. 459, 470.
83. Amnesty International, "Amnesty International's 12-Point Programme for the Prevention of Torture and Other Cruel, Inhuman, or Degrading Treatment or Punishment by Agents of the State," April 21, 2005. www.amnesty.org.
84. Amnesty International, "Amnesty International's 12-Point Programme for the Prevention of Torture and Other Cruel, Inhuman, or Degrading Treatment or Punishment by Agents of the State."
85. Tobias Kelly, "The UN Committee Against Torture: Human Rights Monitoring and the Legal Recognition of Cruelty," *Human Rights Quarterly*, August 2009, p. 781.
86. Quoted in Kelly, "The UN Committee Against Torture," p. 793.
87. Quoted in Kelly, "The UN Committee Against Torture," p. 797.
88. Hawkins, "Release of Torture Report Underscores Need for Accountability."
89. David Cole, "What to Do About the Torturers?," *New York Review of Books*, January 15, 2009. www.nybooks.com.
90. Quoted in Deutshe Welle, "European Human Rights Court Rules on El-Masri Rendition Case," December 13, 2012. www.dw.com.
91. Quoted in Sheri Finkjan, "Judge Allows Lawsuit Against Psychologists in C.I.A. Torture Case," *New York Times*, January 27, 2017. www.nytimes.com.
92. Quoted in Matt Ford, "Remembering Elie Wiesel," *Atlantic*, July 2, 2016. www.theatlantic.com.

How to Get Involved

By getting involved, you can make a difference. Organizations that work to prevent or expose torture often need volunteers for a variety of tasks ranging from letter writing to organizing events. Some organizations also sponsor internships for youth.

Amnesty International

1 Easton St.
London WC1X 0DW
United Kingdom
www.amnesty.org

Founded in 1961, Amnesty International is a nonprofit organization that investigates and exposes human rights abuses around the world. The organization has seven regional offices on four continents as well as offices in seventy different countries. It lobbies countries to stop torture, abolish the death penalty, protect sexual and reproductive rights, and combat discrimination.

Human Rights Foundation (HRF)

350 Fifth Ave., Suite 4202
New York, NY 10118
www.hrf.org

The HRF is a nonpartisan, nonprofit organization that promotes and protects human rights globally, with a focus on closed societies. It focuses its work on the founding ideals of the human rights movement represented in the 1948 Universal Declaration of Human Rights and the 1976 International Covenant on Civil and Political Rights.

Human Rights Watch

350 Fifth Ave., 34th Floor
New York, NY 10118
www.hrw.org

Human Rights Watch is a nonprofit, nongovernmental human rights organization made up of roughly four hundred staff members around the globe. Established in 1978, the organization partners with local human rights groups to lobby governments for changes in policy and practice that promote human rights. It publishes more than one hundred reports annually on human rights in ninety countries.

International Committee of the Red Cross (ICRC)

19 Avenue de la Paix
CH-1202 Geneva
Switzerland
www.icrc.org

Established in 1863, the ICRC operates worldwide, employing sixteen thousand people in more than eighty countries. With a mandate that stems essentially from the Geneva Conventions of 1949, the organization is dedicated to helping people affected by armed conflict and violence and promoting the laws that protect victims of war. The organization has won the Nobel Peace Prize three times.

Office of the United Nations High Commissioner for Human Rights (OHCHR)

Palais Wilson
Palais des Nations
CH-1201 Geneva 10
Switzerland
www.ohchr.org

The OHCHR is the principal human rights office of the United Nations. The office has a workforce of 689 international human rights officers serving in UN peace missions or political offices around the world. The office supports the work of the UN human rights mechanisms, including the treaty bodies, and assists countries in upholding human rights.

World Organisation Against Torture (OMCT)
PO Box 21
8 Rue du Vieux-Billard
CH-1211 Geneva 8
Switzerland
www.omct.org

Created in 1985, the OMCT is a coalition of international nongovernmental organizations fighting against torture, summary executions, enforced disappearances, and all other cruel, inhuman, or degrading treatment. The OMCT has 311 affiliated organizations in its network and thousands of correspondents around the globe.

Youth for Human Rights International (YHRI)
1920 Hillhurst Ave., Suite 416
Los Angeles, CA 90027
www.youthforhumanrights.org

YHRI is a nonprofit organization founded in 2001 to teach youth about human rights and inspire them to become advocates for tolerance and peace. YHRI offers human rights education both in the classroom and in nontraditional educational settings. The organization has hundreds of groups, clubs, and chapters around the world.

For Further Research

Books

Sid Jacobson, *The Torture Report: A Graphic Adaptation*. New York: Nation, 2017.

Joshua E.S. Phillips, *None of Us Were Like This Before: American Soldiers and Torture*. London: Verso, 2012.

Mohamedou Ould Slahi, *Guantánamo Diary*. New York: Little, Brown, 2015.

Rachel Wahl, *Just Violence: Torture and Human Rights in the Eyes of the Police*. Stanford, CA: Stanford University Press, 2017.

Internet Sources

American RadioWorks, "What Killed Sergeant Gray," American Public Media, 2010. http://americanradioworks.publicradio.org /features/vets.

Amnesty International, *Amnesty International Annual Report 2016/17*. www.amnesty.org/en/latest/research/2017/02/amnesty -international-annual-report-201617.

Matt Apuzzo, Sheri Fink, and James Risen, "How U.S. Torture Left a Legacy of Damaged Minds," *New York Times*, October 9, 2016. www.nytimes.com/2016/10/09/world/cia-torture-Guantá namo-bay.html?_r=0.

Association for the Prevention of Torture, *Putting Prevention into Practice*, 2016. www.apt.ch/content/files_res/putting-prevention -into-practice-opcat10.pdf.

Australian Broadcasting Corporation News, "The Forgotten Children: Four Corners Visits Nauru," YouTube, 2016. https://youtu .be/4uakOJL2Esw.

International Committee of the Red Cross, "Geneva Conventions of 1949 and Additional Protocols, and Their Commentaries." https://ihl-databases.icrc.org/applic/ihl/ihl.nsf/vwTreaties1949.xsp.

Istanbul Protocol Project in the Basque Country Working Group, *Incommunicado Detention and Torture in Spain*, 2016. http://tbinternet.ohchr.org/Treaties/CAT/Shared%20Documents/ESP/INT_CAT_CSS_ESP_20098_S.pdf.

Cover: iStockphoto/ABB Photo

About the Author

Bradley Steffens is an award-winning poet, playwright, novelist, and author of more than thirty-five nonfiction books for children and young adults. He is a two-time recipient of the San Diego Book Award for Best Young Adult and Children's Nonfiction: his *Giants* won the 2005 award, and his *J.K. Rowling* claimed the 2007 prize. Steffens also received the Theodor S. Geisel Award for best book by a San Diego County author in 2007.